A Christmas Treasure

GLORIA IN EXCELSIS DEO
Carole Black

Edna McCann

A Christmas Treasure

with original illustrations by Carole Black

HarperCollins*PublishersLtd*

The author greatfully acknowledges the following sources: "Old-Fashioned Christmas" by Edna Jaques. Published in Canada by Thomas Allen & Sons Limited. Reprinted courtesy of the publisher. "To the Years that Used to Be" by Annette Victorin. Reprinted courtesy of the author's estate. "Christmas Card Magic" by Della Adams Leitner. Reprinted courtesy of the author's estate. "Kitchen Memories" by Truda McCoy. Reprinted courtesy of the author's estate.

First Edition

HarperCollins Publishers Ltd. has made every effort to find the holders of copyrighted materials published in this book. Any questions regarding permissions should be addressed to the publisher.

HarperCollins books may be purchased for educational, business, or sales promotional use through our Special Markets Department.

HarperCollins Publishers Ltd.
2 Bloor Street East, 20th Floor
Toronto, Ontario, Canada
M4W 1A8

www.harpercanada.com

National Library of Canada Cataloguing in Publication

McCann, Edna
A Christmas treasure / Edna McCann ; with illustrations by Carole Black. – 1st ed.

ISBN 0-00-639417-5

1. Christmas 2. Christmas cookery.
3. Christmas decorations. I. Title.

GT4985.M23 2003 394.2663 C2003-903769-X

TC 9 8 7 6 5 4 3 2 1

Printed and bound in Canada
Set in Dante

This book is dedicated to my family,
whose love and support make me feel that
it's Christmas every day of the year.

Contents

A Christmas Treasure

A Christmas Welcome

We bring in the holly, the ivy, the pine,
The spruce and the hemlock together we twine;
With evergreen branches our walls we array,
For keeping of Christmas, our high holiday.

Old English Carol

Few holidays are anticipated with more joy and delight than Christmas. It is a season of peace and goodwill, a time to enjoy the love of family and friends and the wealth of customs and traditions that we have come to associate with the birth of Jesus, more than two thousand years ago.

For those of us of the Christian faith around the world, it is a time of giving and receiving, of hope and inspiration—a time to come together in renewed faith and optimism.

In the years that have passed since Christ's birth, Christmas has evolved into a celebration that embraces customs from many countries. I like to think of Christmas as a time that can bind the world together in hope and peace, a time when all of us may say "Joy to the World."

In this book, I hope to capture for you the true meaning of Christmas, with heartwarming stories of love, hope and faith, some shared traditions, and recipes for sumptuous Christmas food. There are ideas, not only for gifts, but also for beautiful wrappings and timeless decorations that I hope will add to your enjoyment of the Yuletide season.

I'd like to open this collection with a story of friends who were very close to my heart.

Many years ago, my husband, George, and I met a wonderful couple with whom we shared a long and treasured friendship. Marion and Neal McDowell became those special people that are such a rare commodity—true friends who share with you all that life sends, both good and bad.

When George passed away, Neal and Marion were two of the first people to arrive, bringing great comfort as well as practical help. Neal assisted me with funeral arrangements, and Marion took charge of feeding the family, a chore that would have completely overwhelmed me at the time.

As the years passed, we continued to stay in close touch, sharing stories of our children and our grandchildren, and so it was with great sorrow that I received a call from Marion in August 1981, telling me that Neal was gravely ill with cancer.

What came after that is well told by Marion and Neal's daughter, Marilyn. I hope you'll enjoy it.

A Very Special Gift

When people learn that my father passed away on Christmas Day, their immediate reaction is one of great dismay. "Doesn't it make Christmas very difficult for you?" they will ask.

Actually, that last Christmas my father spent with us was so special that I look forward each year to the memories December 25 brings to our whole family.

In July 1981, my father suffered a seizure at his cottage in southern Ontario. The ensuing hospitalization and myriad of tests showed that Dad had a walnut-sized brain tumour, and an operation to remove the tumour was scheduled for August 25.

My father, always an optimist, entered the hospital with high hopes of a full recovery from, in his words, "a minor inconvenience."

"Don't worry about me. I'm sure this will turn out well," he said, as he gave the thumbs-up on the way into the operating room.

Only later, when the nurse-liaison came to the waiting room, did we learn that Dad was very concerned about what might happen to him. A man whose IQ placed him in the "gifted or brilliant" category, he had held the nurse's hand and implored, "If I'm to become a burden to my family, please ask the doctor to let me die now," as tears trickled down his cheeks.

The doctor came to us immediately after the operation.

"I'm so terribly sorry, but the news is not good. The tumour is extremely fast-growing and I was able to get only a small portion of it."

Our family sat in stunned silence until I was finally able to blurt out, "What does that mean?"

"I'm afraid that, even with treatment, your father likely has only four to six months to live."

The poor man hardly knew which way to look as he delivered this knockout blow.

The neurologist was a bit more encouraging.

"I've had patients live for two or three years after radiation. Don't give up hope. Your father is an extremely determined man."

In the weeks that followed, Dad endured radiation treatments, weight and hair loss and, most distressing to him, the impairment of his ability to read, write or make himself understood. For someone who had been president of a publishing firm and whose vocabulary was admired by all who knew him, it was a bitter blow.

Unwilling to give up yet, however, he made us understand with gestures and mime that he wanted us to read him the newspaper each day as he worked to build back his strength by riding a stationary bicycle.

By mid-November, when the radiation treatments had given the tumour its maximum reduction, Mom and Dad decided to go to Florida for a much-deserved vacation. It was disastrous.

Dad's symptoms returned almost immediately. Dizzy spells caused him to fall frequently; his speech was again slurred and jumbled. Mom was terrified. It was time to come home. We met them at the airport on the evening of December 11 and took Dad directly to the hospital.

Over the next two weeks, my father would look at me expectantly when I arrived in his hospital room. I would announce the day, the date and the number of days until Christmas. The closer we got to the big day, the greater was his look of relief. He was hanging on tenaciously.

Knowing how much this day meant to Dad, the doctors suggested that he be given a day pass so he could enjoy the day with the family.

The entire family gathered at our home and we greeted Dad joyfully as my husband and my brother helped him in from the car. It was a magical day. Our daughter, Kelly, who had received an art kit as a gift, was having some difficulty drawing a snowy landscape.

"I'll help," said her grandfather clearly.

Kelly turned over her paints and brushes, and Dad, who as a young man had studied at the Ontario College of Art, showed her how to sketch the trees and shade the snow to give depth to her work.

As we opened gifts, Dad had a big smile and an appropriate comment for each one. "Beautiful sweater," "Fine sled, great for the big hill."

He was our father and grandfather of old.

We moved into the dining room for our traditional turkey dinner and, as we took our places, Dad said, "I would like to say the grace."

It was simple but eloquent.

"Thank you, Lord, for allowing us to be together on this blessed Christmas Day. We thank You for our family and friends and all of the happy memories to treasure. Bless this food to our use and us to Thy service. Amen."

There was a moment of electrifying silence, and then it was Christmas dinner as usual. Platters of food were passed as the children laughed and chattered and the adults pronounced the meal delicious with almost every mouthful.

After dinner the children set off to test their sleds at the nearby hill while the adults enjoyed their coffee.

At about 3:30, Dad said, "It's time for me to go."

I explained that his pass allowed him to stay out until much later but he insisted simply, "It's time for me to go, now."

We bundled Dad up in his coat and hat and my mom, my husband and my brother waved to us from the car. They drove past the toboggan hill where the grandchildren, in turn, gave Grandpa a hug and said their goodbyes.

"Bye, Grampa, see you soon." "Bye, Grampa, watch me come down the hill as you leave." "See you later, Grandpa."

Dad made it to the doors of the hospital when his breathing became very laboured. In just a few minutes he was gone.

For me, just as God gave us the gift of His own Son that first Christmas Day, He also gave our family the gift of one more special day with Dad before He called him Home. It was a day filled with joy that we'll remember forever.

In late November, 17 years later, my mother, who had made the devastating downhill slide that the ravages of Parkinson's disease provides, remarked in a casual conversation with me, that if anything were going to happen to her she hoped that she would be with Dad for Christmas.

On December 22 I received the call from the nursing home that I was almost expecting. Mother had had a heart attack in the night, was in a coma and unlikely to live through the day. She slipped away about five o'clock that evening, and we bid our farewells as she was laid to rest beside Dad on the afternoon of Christmas Eve. She, too, was Home for Christmas.

Marilyn Picard

And it was always said of him, that he knew how to keep Christmas well . . . May that be truly said of us, and all of us! And so, as Tiny Tim observed, God bless us, Every One.

Charles Dickens
from "A Christmas Carol"

A Little Christmas History

Now is the season of the holly and the mistletoe; the days are come in which we hang our rooms with the sober green of December and feel it is summer in our hearts.

The Saturday Evening Post
December 29, 1866

The reason for establishing December 25 as Christ's birthday is not known exactly, but it is thought that it was chosen by the Christians to correspond with the pagan festivals around the time of the winter solstice.

Many religious scholars believe that the birth of Jesus Christ, the "light of the world," was celebrated at this time to coincide with the return of longer days, making Christianity more meaningful to the pagans whom the Christians hoped to convert.

The period between December 21 and January 1 was a popular time for festivities. This was when the Vikings held the winter festival of "Juul" (hence the derivation of our term *Yule*) to honour their god, Odin.

The burning of the "Yule log" during the Christmas season is probably part of the winter solstice rite of burning bonfires to celebrate the return of longer days.

Today the bûche de Noël, or Yule Log, is a chocolate cake covered with "snow" (white icing) that symbolizes the Yule log of years past.

The Druids and Romans also had celebrations at this time of year. Our Christmas tradition of decorating with holly, ivy and mistletoe, indulging in eating and drinking, and exchanging gifts may be traced back to "Saturnalia" or the rites of winter solstice. Saturn, the Roman god of agriculture, was honoured to ensure an end to winter and the lengthening of the days—needed for the successful growth of crops. It was a time of charity as well, for the wealthy often presented clothing or money to their poorer friends. The less wealthy presented garlands, candles and incense to their benefactors for the decoration of their homes.

Saturnalia began with religious rites on December 17, and it lasted for seven days. In early times, the only Romans allowed to work during Saturnalia were cooks and bakers, as they were responsible for the feasts—a large part of the celebration.

During this seven-day period, slaves became free men and one man from the group was chosen as "king." The colourful paper hats found in today's

Christmas crackers are thought to symbolize the crown worn by the "king" of the slaves.

As well, homes were often decorated and family members gave each other small gifts. The wonderful tradition of the feasts is with us today as many Christians everywhere celebrate Christ's birth with a family dinner, often the most elaborate of the year.

The decorating of the evergreen, the reenactment of the nativity and the singing of carols are all still a large part of our celebration in the 21st century.

The joining of the Christian and pagan traditions has given us a time of celebration each year that is enjoyed by young and old alike. We hope that it is a time of "peace on earth, goodwill toward men."

Old-Fashioned Christmas

I like old-fashioned things at Christmastime—
Old-fashioned lights and tinsel on a tree,
Red candles lighted in a quiet room,
A grandma with a baby on her knee;

The smell of cedar in the living room,
Pinecones with bits of silver in their tips,
A holly wreath tied with scarlet bow,
The smell of wax when a candle drips,

The taste of mincemeat from a covered crock,
Brown Christmas cake, mulled cider in a jug,
Gay parcels piled behind the Christmas tree,
Warm firelight playing on a crimson rug;

The brown skin of the turkey rich and good,
Old-fashioned dressing made with sage and bread,
Rich gravy spilling from a golden bowl,
Cranberry jelly glowing bright and red,

The mother with the clean print apron on,
Dishing the dinner up with happy pride;
Dad carving turkey, heaping the plates,
Laying the wishbone snugly to one side.

I love old-fashioned things on Christmas Day
Snow on the ground, a church across the way.

Edna Jaques

Advent

Christmas is a loving heart
Since the world began,
Best of all, it is the gift
Of God's own Son to man!

Loraine Good

The fourth Sunday before Christmas marks the beginning of Advent. The term *advent* comes from the Latin *adventus*, which means "a coming" and, for many families, this marks the beginning of the Christmas season.

In some homes, the Sunday before Advent is also a special occasion. Known as "stir-up Sunday," it is the day set aside for making Christmas puddings and fruitcakes and for mixing mincemeat. This tradition comes from the Collect in the Church of England's Book of Common Prayer, which says:

"Stir up, we beseech thee, O Lord, the wills of thy faithful people; that they, plenteously bringing forth the fruit of thy good works, may of thee be plenteously rewarded; through Jesus Christ our Lord."

As the foods are being prepared, every person who comes into the house stirs each pot three times, once each in the name of the Father, Son and Holy Ghost. It is a quaint old practice that has been handed down through many generations.

Christmas Mincemeat

Although most people who enjoy mincemeat tarts or pies find it much simpler to buy tinned mincemeat, there is nothing quite as good as the traditional homemade Christmas mincemeat. This is the recipe my grandmother passed on to us.

8 oz. (250 g) grated suet
Juice plus the grated rind of one orange
Juice plus the grated rind of one lemon
4 oz. (125 g) mixed candied peel, chopped
4 oz. (125 g) blanched almonds, chopped
4 oz. (125 g) candied cherries, chopped
3 oz. (100 g) dried apricots, chopped
3 oz. (100 g) candied ginger, chopped
8 oz. (250 g) currants
½ tsp. (2 mL) salt
½ tsp. (2 mL) grated nutmeg
½ tsp. (2 mL) mixed spice
8 oz. (250 g) brown sugar

2 large green cooking apples, cored, peeled and diced very fine
1 lb. (500 g) sultanas
1 lb. (500 g) raisins
1½ cups brandy

1. In a large bowl, put the suet, orange and lemon rind, mixed peel, almonds, cherries, apricots, ginger, currants, salt, spices, brown sugar, fruit juices and apples. Stir well to combine.
2. Finely chop the sultanas and raisins in a food processor or blender, and add to the bowl. Stir well to break up any lumps that may have formed before adding the brandy. Stir again, then let the mixture stand overnight. Next day stir again very well to blend the fruits thoroughly.
3. Store in clean, sterilized, airtight jars.
   Fill unbaked pie shell with the mincemat, and cover with top crust. Bake at 350°F (180°C) for 45 minutes. We serve warm mincemeat pies and tarts with a dollop of fresh whipped cream. Delicious!

Makes 2 to 3 large pies or 3 dozen tarts.

A number of Advent traditions have come to North America from Europe. Advent wreaths and calendars are two such traditions.

The circular shape of the Advent wreath (which originated with the German Lutherans) symbolizes God's eternal love; the candles are symbolic of Christ as the "Light of the World." The traditional wreath is made of fir, holly or laurel, and one purple candle, denoting royalty, is added to the wreath on each of the four Sundays in Advent. The fifth candle—lit December 24—is the Christ candle and it is white, signifying purity.

The Advent calendar typically shows a Christmas scene incorporating little doors or windows that are opened, one each day, for 24 days preceding Christmas Day. Calendars for children often have pieces of chocolate behind each window and, not surprisingly, they seem to be more popular than most others.

In Scandinavia, the tradition of hanging a wreath of fir or pine boughs on the front door was a sign of welcome to family and friends, and of good luck for the coming year. The wreath, now the most popular of all door decorations, is a gesture of welcome wherever it is hung. Contemporary wreaths are not restricted to evergreen boughs. Pine cones, dried flowers, herbs, fruits and vegetables are just a few of the many types of materials being used to create spectacularly decorative wreaths.

Pine Cone Wreath

One of the prettiest and longest-lasting wreaths is also one of the easiest to make. A pine cone wreath, traditional in Italy, can be made any time during the year and saved from year to year.

MATERIALS

Pine cones of various sizes and shapes
Wire base (purchased at any craft shop)
Fine-gauge floral wire
Hot glue gun
Ribbon of your choice (I find the wire-edged ribbon holds its shape best)
Spray varnish (optional)

Although this wreath may be made without spraying the pine cones, the varnish will help to preserve the wreath for many years.

1. Spray pine cones with varnish and allow to dry thoroughly.
2. Sort pine cones by size.
3. Attach large cones to the wire base with floral wire.
4. Attach medium and smaller cones to the larger ones with hot glue. Continue adding cones until the wreath is at desired fullness.

5. Take a length of the wire-edged ribbon and fashion a bow of desired size. Allow enough ribbon to hang down from the wreath as tails.
6. Using floral wire, attach the bow to the wreath by pushing the floral wire through the cones and securing it to the wire base. You may want to reinforce the attachment by using hot glue on the back of the bow and attaching the bow to the cones.

You can change the wreath each year by wiring in bits of holly with berries, dried baby roses, baby's breath, red peppers, candy canes or brass jingle bells.

To store the wreath from year to year, simply lay it flat in a plastic bag.

If your wreath needs dusting, use a hair dryer on low setting.

Let every hall have boughs of green,
With berries glowing in between,
In the week when Christmas comes.

Eleanor Farjeon

In the past, Advent was a period of fasting, when no meat, cheese or alcoholic drinks could be consumed.

In our family, the first day of Advent was, and still is,

a cause for celebration and a wonderful excuse to enjoy a special meal. Each person chooses a food that they would particularly like to have at this meal. This often leads to a rather unusual combination of foods, but for the children in the family, this is part of what makes the dinner memorable.

Desserts have always been a high priority in our family and anything containing chocolate is eaten with great fervour. My grandson Marshall's wife, Jamie, made a wonderful chocolate mousse for an Advent dinner some years ago and it has become a family favourite.

Chocolate Mousse with Raspberries

1 cup (250 mL) chocolate milk
16 oz. (500 g) semi-sweet chocolate, chopped
1 tsp. (5 mL) vanilla extract
⅔ cup (150 mL) whipping cream
8 chocolate cups (found in most grocery stores)
1 16 oz. (500 g) package of frozen raspberries, thawed
mint leaves for decoration (optional)

1. In a bowl, combine chocolate milk with chocolate. Place bowl over a pot of simmering water. Whisk

until chocolate is melted (about 5 minutes). Stir in vanilla. Remove from heat and cool.

2. Whip cream until stiff peaks form. Fold whipped cream into cooled chocolate mixture.
3. Spoon mousse into chocolate cups, dividing it evenly, and chill for about 4 hours.
4. To serve, spoon thawed raspberries over mousse. Add a sprig of mint, if you like, for decoration.

Makes 8 servings.

The heart goes home at Christmas,
Across the miles and years.
Amid the splendour of the day,
The memories appear.

Alice Leedy Mason

Spending Christmas away from home and family can be very difficult. I like to tell this story of Rolie and Nancy and their Christmas spent in Canada's far north.

A Christmas Shared

It was 1937 and the young minister and his wife were spending their first Christmas in Canada's far north, many hundreds of miles away from their families back on the east coast.

Although they felt very fortunate that Rolie had been posted to a parish of his own, it would be difficult to feel much Christmas spirit so far from home. As well, a minister's salary in those days rarely went beyond the barest necessities—it certainly wouldn't include many decorations or gifts.

Finally, a few days before Christmas, Nan suggested that they could at least cut down a small evergreen in the woods to have for a Christmas tree.

It was a bitterly cold day as they headed off with the sled and an axe with which to chop down a tree. Many neighbours waved from their windows as the couple made their way down the street, their exhaled breaths forming frosty clouds around their faces.

Trees were plentiful, and it wasn't long before Rolie and Nan headed home with a lovely little spruce tree. The tree seemed to buoy their spirits, and soon they were humming their favourite Christmas carols as they dragged the sled back to their tiny home.

They hadn't been indoors long before there came a knock at the door. Rolie opened the door to greet an elderly neighbour.

"I thought maybe you and the missus might be able to use these," he said, handing Rolie a box of exquisite crystal globes for the tree. "We seem to have extras."

"Please come in for a cup of tea," Rolie invited, "and you can help Nan put them on the tree."

Rolie had barely closed the door when another knock brought him back. On the porch stood several other members of the parish, each holding lights or ornaments, all being offered to adorn the small evergreen.

It wasn't long before the house was bulging at the seams with friends and neighbours, each anxious to donate something to the new minister and his wife.

After everyone had left, Nancy found that it was not just decorations that these kind folks had brought. In the kitchen, she discovered plates of cookies, jars of jams and jellies, fruit preserves, potatoes, squash, homemade bread and thick slabs of bacon.

"Their generosity was overwhelming," Nan told me years later. "We enjoyed a wonderful Christmas—probably one as near to the true meaning of the Christmas spirit and sharing as we ever had.

"When we left the north our beautiful decorations came with us and we've used them each and every year. I never look at those decorations that I don't remember how those wonderful people made us feel so welcome and so much less lonely."

George and I had a very similar experience our first Christmas away from home. Thanks to the generosity of our parishioners, we had a beautifully decorated tree. George and I cherished those decorations and they moved with us for many years. I have now given most of them to my daughters and their families, and it gives me great pleasure, when I visit their homes, to see that the decorations we so treasured have places of honour on their trees today.

At Christmas time, these things I know:
Fragrance of pine, air frosted, keen with snow;
Laughter of children, raised in glad surprise;
Breathless expectancy; the smiling eyes
Of friends with gifts white-clad and ribbon-tied;
Odour of good things cooking. There abide
The dearest things I know in all the earth:
Home and the loved ones, friendship, song and mirth

Author Unknown

Many families have tree-decorating parties—a great way to have a family get-together at this time of year. When we decorate our tree, we like to serve a traditional favourite Christmas drink, eggnog. Of course, eggnog is available commercially at most grocery stores, but eggnog can be made quite simply and nothing can match the delicious flavours of the homemade variety.

Eggnog

There are many different recipes for eggnog, but my family prefers this one.

6 eggs, separated
½ to ¾ cup (125 to 175 mL) sugar
3 cups (750 mL) whipping cream
2 cups (500 mL) milk
2 tsp. (10 mL) vanilla extract or rum extract
ground nutmeg for garnish
¼ cup (50 mL) rum (if desired for an adult party)

1. In a large bowl, beat egg whites until stiff but not dry, gradually adding sugar. In another very large bowl, beat egg yolks until they are lemon yellow. Fold the egg whites into the egg yolks.
2. In a third bowl, beat the cream until stiff. Add it to the egg mixture, along with the milk and vanilla, stirring gently. Chill well. Sprinkle with nutmeg just before serving. If adding rum, stir in gently before serving.

Makes 8 6-oz servings.

Pumpkin Eggnog

A nice variation of the usual eggnog recipe adds pumpkin, a favourite flavour in our home.

2 eggs, separated
½ cup (125 mL) sugar
½ cup (125 mL) pumpkin purée
4 cups (1 L) half-and-half cream
¼ cup (50 mL) Jamaican rum (optional for adult party)
pumpkin spice for garnish

1. In a large bowl, beat egg whites until stiff but not dry, gradually adding sugar. In another bowl, beat egg yolks until they are lemon yellow. Beat the pumpkin purée into the egg yolks, then fold the mixture into the egg whites.
2. In a third bowl, beat the cream until frothy. Add it to the egg mixture along with the rum. Stir to blend and chill well. Serve very cold. Sprinkle with a dash of pumpkin spice just before serving. If the eggnog is served to adults, some hosts prefer to increase the amount of rum to 2 cups/500 mL.

Makes 8 6-oz servings.

Now Christmas is come,
Let's beat up the drum,
And call all our neighbours together;
And when they appear,
Let's make them such cheer
As will keep out the wind and the weather.

Washington Irving

The Christmas Tree

O Christmas tree, O Christmas tree,
With happiness we greet you.
When decked with candles once a year,
You fill our hearts with Yuletide cheer.
O Christmas tree, O Christmas tree,
With happiness we greet you.

Old German Carol

Among the many traditional symbols of Christmas, the tree stands out as one of the most important.

Long before the tree was a part of the Christmas celebration, it was associated with pagan ceremonies. During the ancient Roman festival of Saturnalia, evergreen trees, considered to be a symbol of hope because of their ability to survive even the harshest winter conditions, were decorated to honour the continuing circle of life. In northern Europe, Druids honoured their gods by tying tributes to tree branches.

There are many stories of how the evergreen tree

Carole Black

became a part of the Christmas celebration, but the most widely accepted legend relates the story of an English missionary named Winfred, later known as St. Boniface. In the eighth century, when the Christianization of Germany was complete, Winfred chopped down the sacred oak of Odin (a pagan god). Behind the sacred oak stood a small fir tree, which he dedicated to the infant Jesus.

Many years later, Martin Luther, a founder of the Protestant faith, was walking in the woods late one evening when he saw the stars twinkling through the boughs of the evergreen trees. He was so enchanted by the sight that he went home and attempted to recreate the spectacle for his children by placing small lighted candles all over the tree. The lights were symbolic of the heavens from where Christ came.

The Christmas tree with candles gleaming
A glow is kindling in all our hearts,
It speaks of God's pure love-light streaming
It brings us hope and joy imparts.

Traditional German Carol

In the early 1600s, a visitor to Strasbourg, Germany, wrote of fir trees set up in the parlours of many homes. These trees were decorated with apples, cookies, candies and paper roses. This custom seems to have spread throughout Germany and then northward to the Scandinavian countries.

Queen Charlotte, wife of George III, set up a tree at Windsor Castle in 1789, but it was not until the 1840s when Prince Albert, consort to Queen Victoria, began importing fir trees from his native Coburg that the British public took up the fashion. When the *Illustrated London News* published a picture of the royal family gathered around their tree at Windsor Castle, the people of Britain were quick to adopt the custom.

The tradition spread quickly to North America and in 1882, the first American Christmas tree lit with electric lights thrilled the people of New York City. The original Christmas bulbs were simply smaller versions of the household light bulb (invented by Thomas Edison in 1879). As tree lights became less expensive, they became common and took many shapes and forms. In the 1920s, lights in the shape of birds and fruit were popular. In the 1930s miniature bulbs and bulbs that flashed were fashionable.

In the 1940s and 1950s the "bubble light" gained a popularity unprecedented in the history of Christmas lighting. Noma Lighting of New York first marketed these little gems in 1945, and within a few years there were nearly 30 different types of bubble on the market. Although bubble lights are still manufactured today, they really can't compete with those of yesteryear.

For some years, artificial trees became quite popular in North America; however, the evergreen has since returned to its number one ranking.

Originally, decorations for Christmas trees were foodstuffs or paper, with Christmas roses, apple slices or popcorn strings enjoying great popularity. Later in the 19th century, ornaments became more elaborate. Exquisite crystal balls, gold and silver stars, hand-crafted fabric ornaments or hand-carved wooden decorations were *de rigueur*. People paid enormous sums of money to acquire these decorative treasures. Many of the antique decorations are almost priceless today.

To the Years that Used to Be

The shining, sparkling ornaments
Strung on our Christmas tree,
Reach out and take me by the hand
To the years that used to be:

I am a little girl once more,
Our tree wears candlelights,
We sing the song the angels sang
And thrill to simple sights.

A star tops our small Christmas tree,
Red apples hug each bough,

Long strings of popcorn and bright chains . . .
(If those days were here now!)

Grampa tells us of the Three Wise Men
Who came to Bethlehem,
I dream a little girlish dream
In which I follow them.

The shining, sparkling ornaments
Strung on our Christmas tree,
Reach out and take me by the hand
To years that used to be!

Annette Victorin

We are lucky enough to live in an area where we are able to choose and cut our Christmas tree at one of the many tree farms. Since tree selection in our family is a very time-consuming affair—we look over every tree grown on the property before making our choice—we like to have a winter picnic at the farm. And since the majority of people purchasing trees are in "It's so cold, let's just grab a tree and go home" mode, our family of picnickers often raises a few eyebrows.

Winter picnics are really quite lovely. Today's vacuum jugs can ensure a hot meal, no matter how many hours you plan to be outdoors. Warm clothing and a sheltered area in which to eat make a winter picnic a true delight. The following recipes are several of our winter favourites.

Wild Mushroom Soup

2¼ cups (550 mL) hot water
½ oz. (15 g) dried mushrooms
2 tbsp. (30 mL) unsalted butter
1 cup (250 mL) finely chopped onion
3 cloves garlic, minced
1 lb. (500 g) fresh white mushrooms, sliced
4 oz. (100 g) fresh shiitake mushrooms (stems removed) thinly sliced
⅓ cup (75 mL) all-purpose flour
2¼ cups (550 mL) beef broth
1 small bay leaf
1¼ cups (300 mL) milk
salt to taste
1½ tsp. (7 mL) pepper
chopped chives for additional garnish

1. Soak the dried mushrooms in the hot water for about an hour.
2. In a large saucepan, melt the butter. Add the chopped onion and sauté for 5 minutes. Add garlic and cook for 1 minute.
3. Reserving the liquid, add the dried mushrooms to the onion and garlic mixture. Add remaining mushrooms, cover and cook for about 12 minutes or until the mushrooms release their liquid.
4. Strain the reserved liquid through a double layer of cheesecloth in a sieve over a bowl.
5. Stir flour into the mushroom mixture; cook, stirring continuously, for 2 minutes.
6. Add strained liquid, broth and bay leaf to the mixture. Cover and simmer over low heat for about 25 minutes.
7. Discard bay leaf. Stir in milk, salt and pepper. Simmer, uncovered, for 5 minutes. Serve with a sprinkling of chopped chives (if desired).

Makes 8 servings.

Herbed Cottage Biscuits

Rolls are a wonderful addition to any picnic. Served with wedges of old cheddar cheese, these herbed cottage biscuits are simple but delicious.

3 cups (750 mL) self-rising flour
1 cup (250 mL) finely ground cornmeal
1 tsp. (5 mL) baking powder
1 tsp. (5 mL) dried thyme
1 tbsp. (15 mL) fresh parsley, finely chopped or 1 tsp. (5 mL) parsley flakes
dash each salt and pepper
¾ to 1 cup (185 to 250 mL) milk
2½ oz. (70 g) melted butter

1. Combine flour, cornmeal and baking powder with the thyme, parsley, salt and pepper. Add milk and mix to a scone-like dough.
2. Pour the melted butter into a small bowl. Divide the dough into walnut-sized balls and roll each ball in the melted butter. Place the balls in a greased round cake pan. Continue until all dough balls have been coated and are evenly spaced in the pan. Pour any remaining butter over the dough balls.

3. Bake in a pre-heated 450°F (230°C) oven for 25 minutes or until the tops are golden brown. Pull rolls apart and serve with butter and wedges of old cheddar cheese.

Hot Mocha Milk

Hot drinks are essential for any winter picnic. Hot mocha milk is loved by young and old alike.

½ cup (125 mL) instant coffee powder
⅔ cup (150 mL) Nestlé's chocolate-flavoured drink mix
½ cup (125 mL) sugar
10 cups (2.5 L) very hot milk

In a heatproof pitcher, mix coffee powder, chocolate drink mix and sugar. Add milk and stir until well combined. Put in a vacuum thermos that has been previously heated with hot water.

Serves 10 generously.

Choose wisely then, each ornament
And frosted tinsel skein
For branches that have worn jewels
Of gleaming mountain rain.

Elizabeth-Ellan Long

When my sister, Sarah, and my brother, Ben, and I were young, we enjoyed making decorations for our tree. The easiest of these to make were popcorn or cranberry chains. Mother would bring in bowls of corn that she had popped, along with containers of cranberries, string and darning needles. We would spend hours stringing popcorn, cranberries or a mixture of both on strings that were long enough to make loops when they were hung on the tree. Mother's criterion for a good chain was simple; the popcorn or cranberries needed to be close enough that the string did not show through.

After Christmas, we would put the chains on the trees in our yard and watch the many birds that would come to feed on them.

Other decorations that we children loved to make were "Good Luck Walnuts." Over the years I taught my children, grandchildren and great-grandchildren how to make these little fortune tellers and we've all enjoyed them.

Good Luck Walnuts

We chop the nutmeats to use in cooking or on ice-cream sundaes that are a treat at our "decoration making" party. You may think of other ways to use the nutmeats.

MATERIALS

English walnuts
A small, sharp-pointed knife
Strips of paper, about ½" (1 cm) wide and 3" to 4" (8 to 10 cm) long
White glue
Pieces of red, green or white, thin wool about 6" (15 cm) long each
Paint and brushes, and/or glitter in various colours

1. Using the sharp knife, open each walnut shell along the seam (this job is best done by an adult). Children may then carefully remove the nutmeat from the shells, taking care not to break the shells. Keep nutmeats in a bowl for later.
2. On the piece of paper, children write good luck wishes or "fortunes" as one would find in Chinese fortune cookies. (Younger children may need help with this.)

3. Roll up one wish and place it in one shell half. Tie a knot in one end of a piece of wool and place the knot inside the round end of the shell (there is a small hole in the round end that will accommodate the wool).
4. Pick up the other half of the shell and dab glue along the flat edge of the shell seam. Do not use too much glue or the shell will be hard to open. Glue the two shell halves together being sure that the fortune and the wool knot are inside the shell.
5. When the glue holding the shells together has dried, the shells may be decorated. The children might wish to paint the shells or, after dabbing glue on the sides, the shells can be dipped in containers of glitter. When they have dried, tie the strings around branches of the tree to hang them. On Christmas Day, family and friends are invited to choose their "Good Luck Walnut."

Christmas is a golden chain that binds a family in faith, hope and love . . . drawing each to the open hearth of togetherness.

Juanita Johnson

Christmas tree ornaments and decorations are many and varied, some especially treasured as they have been handed down through the generations. Decorations also vary according to the country of origin; for example, ornaments made of straw abound in Poland to symbolize thanksgiving for the harvest and hope for good things to come in the new year. Eggs, which are symbolic of future prosperity, are also used as tree ornaments. The eggs have a pin hole poked in each end and then the contents are gently blown out. The shells may be painted or burnished with gold leaf. To hang the shells, glue beads on the end of the egg with model cement and then thread the cord through the bead and tie to make a loop that will fit over the tree branches.

Good friends of mine have found a special way of decorating their tree. Martha collected a number of tiny picture frames—many from the local dollar store—and in the frames she placed pictures of family members, friends and neighbours. The frames were then hung on the tree with red velvet ribbons, interspersed with the other ornaments. Guests in their home delight in finding "their" picture ornament.

In Japan, there is a legend that says if a person folds a thousand paper cranes, the gods may grant that person's wish. These cranes are a symbol of peace. Each year in New York City's Cathedral Church of St. John the Divine, Christmas trees called "peace trees" are decorated with these beautiful origami cranes.

The legend of the Christmas spider comes from Ukrainian and German lore and explains how tinsel became part of our Christmas tree decorating. In this tale, there was a poor widow who had no money for lavish gifts or decorations. Instead, she decorated the tree with what little she had—fruit and nuts. After she went to bed, spiders crawled all over the tree, spinning their webs as they went. When Father Christmas came to visit and saw the delicate lacework that the spiders had created, he turned their webs into silver. The family awoke to a tree that was a sparkling miracle.

Families today still use tinsel to add a sparkle and, in many German and Ukrainian homes, a silver spider and web adorn the tree as a reminder of this story.

Hooray! Hooray! for Christmas Day,
And Christmas trees so bright and gay.
Though sad the trees soon disappear,
The gifts beneath may last for years!

D. L. Gibbs

Christmas Song

Above the weary waiting world,
Asleep in chill despair,
There breaks a sound of joyous bells
Upon the frosted air.
And o'er the humblest roof top, lo,
A star is dancing in the snow.
What makes the yellow star to dance
Upon the brink of night?
What makes the breaking dawn to glow
So magically bright
And all the earth to be renewed
With infinite beatitude?
The singing bells, the throbbing star,
The sunbeams on the snow,
And the awakening heart that leaps
New ecstasy to know.
They are all dancing in the morn
Because a little Child is born.

Bliss Carman

It is often said that the best gift to give is something of yourself. Janet Metcalfe knows this to be true as she remembers Christmas in 1966.

A Gift Remembered

In December 1966, I was a young teacher working at St. Patrick's Mission Teacher Training College in Rhodesia (now Zimbabwe). My friend Vicki (a physiotherapist) and I had been in Africa for two years but were to have been back home in Canada before Christmas. Unfortunately, because of the government's Unilateral Declaration of Independence, and the resulting political uncertainty, the mission had been unable to replace either of us so we agreed to extend our stay for a few more months. Since mail from Africa to Canada took many weeks, and our decision to stay had been a very recent one, our families and friends had not known to send any cards or gifts.

It was customary for the staff and students at the schools, and all but a few essential staff members of the hospital, to go home and spend Christmas with their families. The past two Christmases had been fun, despite our homesickness, because there had been several English missionaries for company. This year Vicki and I were the only non-Africans there and the mission was virtually deserted.

We were both well aware that there is much more to Christmas than cards, gifts and company, but we were feeling very homesick and lonely on that Christmas

Eve. We decided to go for a walk to cheer ourselves up and were surprised to see a car approach, let off a passenger, and then turn and head back toward town. When we got closer, we saw that it was a friend and fellow teacher, Sophie Moyo. She explained that she had been at home in Bulawayo, Zimbabwe, and, thinking of us, far from home and very nearly alone, she had decided to make the long bus trip back and hitch a ride to St. Patrick's to spend Christmas with us. She had also stopped off in town to pick up the mail. Included was a package for us from a friend in Canada who didn't know that we should have been on our way home. She had sent us Canadian maple syrup and sugar. Later that night the three of us went to church and sang carols in Sindebele. Christmas morning we made an enormous stack of pancakes. Sophie tasted maple syrup for the first time, and Vicki and I tasted "home."

The package from Canada was a wonderful present, but the best gift, the one that still brings tears to my eyes, was Sophie's amazingly generous gift of herself.

Janet Metcalfe

What is Christmas? It is a tenderness for the past, courage for the present, hope for the future. It is a fervent wish that every cup may overflow with blessings rich and eternal, and that every path may lead to peace.

Agnes M. Pharo

Christmas Cards

When Christmas rush is over
how good it seems to take
Time to re-read and ponder;
then memories awake
To bring us close together,
forgetting years have passed;
O Christmas cards, your magic
makes Christmas spirit last.

Della Adams Leitner

Christmas cards are a favourite way to keep in touch with good friends and to send best wishes during the holiday season. Cards bring joy to all those who receive them. No matter the picture or the note included, each card says "You are thought of."

Greetings of the New Year were sent out as far back as the early 1400s. It was some time later that letters of Christmas news, blessings and good cheer were dispatched to faraway friends and isolated family members or clergy.

In the 15th century, Germans frequently presented

seasonal gifts, a sort of greeting card with a devotional picture. Often it was a scroll with a picture of the Christ Child bearing a cross that held the inscription "A Good and Blessed Year."

When Sir Rowland Hill reformed the British Postal Service in 1840, it became much easier and less expensive to send cards and letters by mail. During the next few years, Sir Henry Cole, a printer employed by Queen Victoria, sent cards with Christmas greetings to many of his friends. The idea caught the attention of the Queen and her husband, Prince Albert. John Callcott Horsely, a member of the Royal Academy, and a respected illustrator of the day, was commissioned by H.R.H. to design a Christmas card. The card, decorated with vine leaves and showing people drinking a cup of good cheer, was lithographed, hand-tinted and, in 1846, sold a thousand copies at a shilling apiece.

In the United States, the late 1800s saw a great boom in the penny postcard, an inexpensive way to send greetings to those relatives and friends who had moved west.

At the turn of the century, "real photo" postcards came into fashion, frequently showing children dressed in winter clothing and sledding outdoors.

In the early 1900s, card companies such as Rustcraft, Hallmark and, in Canada, Carlton, began producing the first cards to be sent in envelopes. From that time to the present, Christmas cards have become a multi-million-dollar business as people all around the world send greetings to friends and family.

In today's high-tech world, many people choose to send e-mail cards. I am old-fashioned enough to want to send a traditional card and, as I like to add a personal note or letter in each, it takes many hours of preparation before my cards are ready to go.

To save myself some time and energy on those early December days when I am preparing my cards, I like to plan meals that are quick and easy. I make some dishes in advance, then re-heat them—they're great time savers.

Soups and casseroles make warm and satisfying quick-fix lunches or dinners. Here are a few of my favourites to try.

Baked Tuna Noodle Casserole

If your family is not fond of tuna, substitute cooked chicken in this recipe.

1 pkg. (12 oz./340 g) broad egg noodles
4 cups (1 L) broccoli florets
2 cans water-packed tuna (drained)
1 can condensed cream of mushroom soup

1 cup (250 mL) milk
¼ cup (50 mL) grated Parmesan cheese
¼ tsp. (1 mL) coarsely ground black pepper
1 tbsp. (15 mL) butter or margarine
1 pkg. (12 oz./340 g) sliced mushrooms
3 cloves garlic, minced (or 1½ tsp./7 mL minced commercial garlic)
½ cup (125 mL) canned French fried onions

1. Preheat oven to 350°F (180°C). Cook noodles according to package directions, adding broccoli during the last 2 minutes of cooking time. Drain; return to pot. Stir in tuna, soup, milk, cheese and pepper; set aside.
2. In a large skillet melt butter over medium high heat. Add mushrooms and cook until golden and tender, about 5 minutes. Add garlic and cook about 1 minute more. Stir mushroom-garlic mixture into the noodle mixture. Transfer into a greased 2½ quart (2.5 L) baking dish. Sprinkle with fried onions and bake until heated through, about 15 minutes.

Makes 6 servings.

Rice with Chicken and Sausage Bake

2 tbsp. (30 mL) olive oil
1 lb. (500 g) boneless chicken thighs (skin on)
1 large onion, chopped
1 large green pepper, chopped
2 cloves minced garlic (or 1 tsp. / 5 mL commercial minced garlic)
½ lb. (250 g) kielbasa cut into ¼" (5 mm) slices
1 cup (250 mL) uncooked rice
1 can chicken broth (14.5 oz. / 400 mL)
2 tbsp. (30 mL) fresh parsley

1. Preheat oven to 350°F (180°C). In a large, oven-proof skillet, heat oil over medium heat. Add chicken; cook until browned (2 to 3 minutes per side).
2. Remove chicken from skillet, and set aside. In same skillet put chopped onion, pepper and garlic. Cook until they begin to soften (about 5 minutes). Add kielbasa; cook, stirring until sausage browns (4 to 5 minutes).
3. Add rice and broth to skillet. Stir. Return chicken to skillet, cover and bake until the liquid has been absorbed, the rice is tender and the chicken is no

longer pink in the centre (about 40 minutes). Sprinkle with fresh parsley before serving.

Makes 6 servings.

Tomato Orange Soup

This soup is delightfully different and a family favourite.

4 cups (1 L) chicken stock (or low sodium chicken broth)
1 can (28 oz./796 mL) whole peeled tomatoes with juices
1 large onion, thinly sliced
1 large carrot, thinly sliced
1 tsp. (5 mL) grated lemon peel
2 bay leaves
½ tsp. (2 mL) sugar
3 tbsp. (45 mL) butter
2 tbsp. (30 mL) all-purpose flour
¼ cup (50 mL) orange juice
salt and pepper
Croutons

1. Combine stock, tomatoes with juices, onion, carrot, lemon peel, bay leaves and sugar in a large heavy saucepan. Bring to a boil over high heat,

breaking up tomatoes with a spoon. Reduce heat to medium-low and simmer until the vegetables are very tender (about 40 minutes).

2. In a small saucepan over medium heat melt butter. Add flour, and stir 2 minutes. Add 1 cup (250 mL) soup and stir until smooth. Return the mixture to remaining soup in the large saucepan. Simmer until soup thickens, stirring occasionally (about 4 minutes). Remove and discard bay leaves. Working in batches, purée soup in a blender. Return soup to saucepan. Stir in orange juice. Season to taste with salt and pepper.

Soup may be prepared 1 day ahead. Cover and refrigerate.

Before serving, bring to a simmer and serve hot. Sprinkle soup with croutons.

Makes 6 servings.

Many of us have varied taste in Christmas cards, but my daughter Julia came up with what I think is a delightful idea for a card that her friends have come to cherish.

Over the year, Julia takes her camera with her whenever she goes to visit friends and takes pictures of her friends and their families at different occasions. In November she gathers the many photos she has accumulated and selects her favourite for each of her special friends. She then mounts each photo on a plain card that she has purchased at a craft store. She adds a decorative touch by drawing an appropriate seasonal symbol such as holly or snowflakes on the border surrounding the picture. Under each photo she prints, using a calligraphy pen, "Merry Christmas" and the year. Her friends often frame these cards, which offer a yearly reminder of a friendship that continues to grow.

Christmas Card Magic

The Christmas cards and letters
with messages of cheer
Renew the bonds of friendship
neglected through the year.
They bring a sense of nearness,
a unity that gives
A oneness of the spirit
in fellowship that lives.

The crowded days of duties
return with stern demand,
But somehow they are lightened

because we understand
That others care and keep us
within their hearts and prayers,
As we in turn remember,
so each a blessing shares.

And so we come again to Christmas with all its colour and joy, its magic and wonder, its spirit of good will and warmth. But how do we come to Christmas? What it means to us depends on what we bring to it, not in gifts and outer display, but in the inner offerings of love and faith that abide in the heart.

Esther Baldwin York

Gifts from the Kitchen

Early in December is a good time to think about gifts that you may wish to give from your kitchen. A homemade gourmet gift provides a special personal touch that is so appreciated today when many people seem to have little time to spend in the kitchen. Even the most exclusive shops cannot provide that certain special something that comes from any present you have made yourself.

Airtight decorative containers are inexpensive and easy to find in department stores or specialty shops. Add a festive ribbon and you have a gift that both young and old will appreciate.

Another idea is to invite several friends for a cookie exchange party. Each person provides several dozen homemade cookies and gets to choose from many different selections to take home a variety to serve during the holiday season. This is especially nice as it means each person need only bake one type of cookie, a definite time saver. It's important to include the recipes when sharing, as there are those who are on a restricted diet or have severe allergies.

If you want to make a very special gift, buy a picnic hamper and, after lining it with Christmas material, add any number of the homemade gifts. Put in paper plates, napkins, evergreen branches and coloured Christmas balls before wrapping it in cellophane and tying with a large bow. It is a spectacular present.

Shortbread Cookies

Shortbread cookies are favourites of nearly everyone during the Yuletide season. This is the recipe that my family loves.

1 cup (250 mL) butter, softened
3 tbsp. (45 mL) cornstarch
¼ cup (50 mL) granulated sugar
1¾ cup (425 mL) all purpose flour

1. In a large bowl beat the butter until fluffy; gradually beat in the cornstarch and sugar. Using a wooden spoon, add flour to the mixture about ¼ cup (50 mL) at a time, until well mixed.
2. On a lightly floured surface or pastry cloth, roll out dough to a thickness of about ¼" (5 mm). Using cookie cutters of your choice, cut out cookies.

3. Place cookies on waxed paper–lined trays; prick each cookie three times with a fork. Freeze until firm. (If you choose, you can prepare the shortbread to this point, transfer to freezer bags and store for up to 1 month before baking.)
4. Place frozen cookies on a baking sheet. Bake in a preheated oven at 275°F (140°C) for 40 to 50 minutes or until firm to the touch. Remove and let cool on racks. Shortbread can be stored in airtight containers for up to 2 weeks.

Makes 24 cookies.

Cornflake Cookies

My dear friend Mildred Funston provides this next cookie recipe. Although I have given this recipe before, many people have written to me asking that it be included again.

1 cup (250 mL) butter, at room temperature
1 cup (250 mL) white sugar
1 egg, lightly beaten
1 tsp. (5 mL) vanilla
1½ cups (375 mL) all-purpose flour
1 tsp. (5 mL) cream of tartar

½ tsp. (2 mL) salt
1 tsp. (5 mL) baking soda
5 cups (1.25 L) crushed cornflakes

1. Cream butter. Add sugar, egg and vanilla; mix well.
2. Stir in flour, cream of tartar, salt and baking soda. Add cornflakes and mix together.
3. Drop by spoonfuls 2 inches (5 cm) apart on an ungreased cookie sheet. Bake for 10 minutes at 325°F (160°C).

Makes about 3 dozen.

Christmas Bell Cookies

These cookies can be stored in airtight containers for up to one week, or frozen for up to 3 months.

⅔ cup (150 mL) butter (or margarine) at room temperature
¾ cup (175 mL) sugar
1 large egg
1 tsp. (5 mL) grated orange rind
1 tsp. (5 mL) vanilla extract
2 cups (500 mL) all-purpose flour

1½ tsp. (7 mL) baking powder
30 maraschino cherries, cut in half

1. Beat butter at medium speed with an electric mixer, until creamy; gradually add sugar, beating well. Add egg, orange rind and vanilla, beating just until blended.
2. Stir together flour and baking powder; add to butter mixture, beating at low speed until blended. Cover dough and chill for 30 minutes.
3. Shape dough into two 8-inch (20 cm) logs and seal in plastic wrap. Chill dough for at least 8 hours.
4. Cut logs into ¼" (5 mm) slices and place on an ungreased baking sheet. Place a cherry half at the bottom edge of each slice; fold sides, overlapping and slightly covering the cherry to resemble a bell.
5. Bake at 350°F (180°C) for 10 minutes and remove to cool on wire racks.

Makes 5 dozen.

Kitchen Memories

In memory, I often go
Back to the time, when I
Basked in the warm and cheerful glow
In a kitchen filled with pie
And cake, my mother baked . . .
And I can see her smile,
As when the fiery coals she raked,
In good old country style.

I see her stoke the fire with wood,
And slice the ham to fry;
I see the rug on which she stood
Handmade with homemade dye;

I hear the little song she sang
Half to herself, and yet . . .
I knew her carols somehow rang
Where heaven's angels met.

I see again the checkered spread
Of red and white; I see
Dressed turkey and the brown corn bread
And chicken fricassee.

I smell the tantalizing smells;
They'll evermore remain
As long as chiming Christmas bells
Make me a child again.

Truda McCoy

Individual Christmas puddings are an excellent gift. In Victorian times, it was the custom to wrap silver charms in bits of paper and hide them in the pudding. These charms had special names: Bell of Betrothal, Thimble of Blessedness, Wishbone, Coin of Fortune, Bachelor's Button and the Horseshoe of Luck. Today people often hide wrapped coins in the pudding but, if you do, be sure to inform the recipient. (Dentists don't usually work to repair broken teeth on Christmas Day.)

The traditional Christmas pudding is the British plum pudding, but there are many delicious variations of this dessert.

Christmas Pudding

I think you'll enjoy this pudding that adds apricot and apple for a little different flavour.

1 cup (250 mL) seeded raisins
¾ cup (175 mL) currants
¾ cup (175 mL) craisins (dried cranberries)
½ cup (125 mL) chopped mixed candied peel
⅓ cup (75 mL) chopped dried apricots
¼ cup (50 mL) coarsely grated orange rind
1½ cups (375 mL) all purpose flour
1 tsp. (5 mL) baking soda
1 tsp. (5 mL) cinnamon
½ tsp. (2 mL) salt
½ tsp. (2 mL) nutmeg
¼ tsp. (1 mL) allspice
½ cup (125 mL) butter, softened
1¼ cups (300 mL) packed brown sugar
1 cup (250 mL) grated peeled carrots
1 cup (250 mL) grated peeled apples
2 tbsp. (30 mL) orange juice (or orange liqueur)

1. In a bowl mix together the first 6 ingredients. In a separate bowl, stir together flour, baking soda and the spices; sprinkle about one-quarter of the dry mixture over the fruit mixture and toss slightly. Set aside.
2. In a large bowl, cream the butter and sugar together, beating until light and fluffy. Stir in half of the remaining flour mixture. Add the carrots

and apples. Stir in the orange juice, then the remaining flour mixture. Stir in the fruit mixture just until combined.

3. Pour batter into a greased 6-cup (1.5-L) pudding bowl or small individual moulds, filling about two-thirds full, and cover tightly with foil wrap.
4. Steam puddings in boiling water for 2½ to 3 hours for a large pudding, 1 to 2 hours for small moulds (or until cake tester inserted into the centre comes out clean). Let cool thoroughly. Loosen the edge with a knife; turn out and wrap first in plastic wrap and then in attractive gift paper.

Makes 6 servings.

May Your Christmas Be Blessed

May your Christmas be blessed
With joys of old,
Filling the heart with gifts untold.
Friends at the doorway
Bustling good cheer,
Carolers singing the songs we hold dear.
May your Christmas be blessed
With the homiest things,
The warmth of the hearth, a kettle that sings,

A snug little house with loved ones near,
And a heart filled with blessings
To last throughout the year.

Mildred L. Jarrell

Friends appreciate your practical gifts and with a little imagination you can come up with inexpensive but thoughtful presents that will be remembered long after the tinsel and holly have been put away.

Garlic Croutons

Croutons in a glass jar with a small metal scoop attached and a ribbon make a nice hostess gift.

1 cup (250 mL) butter or margarine, melted
4 cloves garlic, pressed
1 loaf French bread, cut into 1" (2.5 cm) cubes
¾ cup (175 mL) grated Parmesan cheese

1. Stir together melted butter and garlic. Toss bread cubes with butter mixture and spread in two lightly greased 10 × 15 inch (30 × 40 cm) jelly-roll pans.
2. Bake at 250°F (120°C) for 1 hour or until golden, stirring every 15 minutes.
3. Sprinkle immediately with cheese, stirring to coat; cool. Store in an airtight container in refrigerator.

Makes 8 cups (2 L).

Beer Muffin Mix

Another thoughtful hostess gift is Beer Muffin Mix. Marg often packs the dry mix in a small basket lined with a Christmas napkin and 1 12-oz. bottle of beer (all the ingredients necessary to make 1 dozen muffins).

4 cups (1 L) commercial biscuit mix
2 tbsp. (30 mL) sugar
3 tbsp. (45 mL) cornmeal

1. Combine all ingredients; place in a heavy duty plastic bag (such as a freezer bag) and store until ready to use. Makes 4½ cups (1.25 L).
2. Gift card Directions: Stir together muffin mix and 1 12-oz. (340-mL) bottle (or can) of beer (at room temperature). Spoon batter into greased 12-muffin pan or 2 6-muffin pans.
3. Bake at 400°F (200°C) for 20 minutes or until golden.

Makes 1 dozen muffins.

For many years I have collected a variety of glass bottles and jars. I use them to make vinaigrette or the popular herb oils. Interesting jars and bottles may also be found at antique or collectible shops in most areas.

Larger grocery stores across North America now stock fresh herbs year round. Almost any herbs may be used, but I have found that basil, dill, rosemary and thyme are most successful.

Rinse the herbs in running water. Shake off the excess water, then lay them to dry on paper towels.

Wash the jars and bottles thoroughly (sterilization is not necessary).

Place the herbs in the jars or bottles, fill with olive oil or sunflower oil and seal tightly. Corks for small-necked bottles may be found in craft stores. Let bottles sit at least two weeks before using.

Vinaigrette

Sometimes I send out these bottles as gifts. If you do, you should write on the card: Serve as dressing over mixed salad greens or pasta salad. For beef or pork marinade stir together equal parts vinaigrette and soy sauce.

⅔ cup (150 mL) vegetable oil
¼ cup (50 mL) white vinegar

¼ (50 mL) cup water
1 clove garlic, pressed
1½ tsp. (7 mL) salt
1 tsp. (5 mL) dried Italian seasoning
1½ tsp. (7 mL) freshly ground pepper

Combine all ingredients in a jar. Cover tightly and shake well.

Makes 1 cup (250 mL).

Then let the holly red be hung,
And all the sweetest carols sung,
While we with joy remember them—
The journeyers to Bethlehem.

F. D. Sherman

If you are looking for a very special gift, there is nothing that friends will welcome more than Chocolate Truffles. This recipe, which comes from my dear friend Peggy who lives in the Cotswold hills in southwest England, makes truffles that chocolate lovers will rave about for months.

Chocolate Truffles

When presenting these truffles as a gift, line a simple box with gold foil and trim it with Christmas ribbon to make a luxury gift that all will welcome.

5 tbsp. (75 mL) whipping cream
8 oz. (250 g) (plus 12 oz./340 g optional for coating) milk chocolate, broken into small pieces
1 to 2 tbsp. (15 to 30 mL) cognac (optional)
4 tbsp. (60 mL) cocoa powder (for dusting)

1. Pour cream into a small saucepan and heat gently until tepid. Put 8 oz. (250 g) of chocolate pieces into a small bowl and melt gently over hot but not boiling water, stirring occasionally. (Do not overheat the chocolate. It must just melt.)
2. When the chocolate has melted, remove the bowl from the hot water. Slowly pour in the cream in a gentle trickle, stirring thoroughly to mix.
3. Let the mixture cool a little and add cognac (if using it). Using a hand whisk or an electric beater on low speed, beat until the mixture becomes lighter in colour and stands in peaks (about 3 to 4 minutes). Refrigerate for about 20 minutes or until stiff.
4. Sprinkle the cocoa powder through a sieve onto a

cookie sheet. Remove spoonfuls of the chocolate paste and roll into balls about 1 inch (2.5 cm) in diameter. Drop each ball onto the cocoa powder and roll to cover. Refrigerate until the balls are firm. You can place them in the freezer until hard but not frozen.

5. If you want to cover the powdered balls in chocolate, melt the remaining 12 oz (340 g) of chocolate over hot water as before. Using a thin wooden skewer, spear each ball and dip it into the melted chocolate, making sure that it is well covered. Place on tinfoil and refrigerate until hardened. Place truffles individually in candy cups (available at most grocery stores), and store in an airtight container until serving. Truffles can be refrigerated up to 1 week or frozen up to 3 months.

Makes 16 truffles.

One of my son-in-law Bruce's favourite desserts is a scoop of ice cream with Brandied Fruit Sauce. Easy to make—it takes only about five minutes—this sauce is also versatile: fold it into whipped cream, or use it as a topping for pudding or crepes.

Brandied Fruit Sauce

If you're giving the sauce as a gift, cut out a circle of Christmas fabric to cover the lid and tie it on with a ribbon.

1 cup (250 mL) chopped mixed candied peel
1 cup (250 mL) red candied cherries, quartered
1 cup (250 mL) dark seedless raisins
¼ cup (250 mL) diced preserved ginger
3 each whole allspice and cloves
1 stick cinnamon, broken into pieces
1 to 1½ cups (250 to 375 mL) brandy or rum

1. In a sterilized 4 cup (1 L) jar, stir together candied peel, cherries, raisins and ginger until mixed well.
2. Tie allspice, cloves and cinnamon in cheesecloth and bury in fruit mixture. Pour in brandy (or rum) until fruit is covered. Seal and store in cool, dark place for 4 days.
3. Remove and discard spice bag. Spoon sauce into gift jars. Seal tightly. Sauce may be stored in a cool, dark, dry place for up to 3 months.

Makes about 3 cups (750 mL).

What can I give Him,
Poor as I am?
If I were a shepherd,
I would give him a lamb;
If I were a wise man,
I would do my part.
But what can I give Him?
Give Him my heart!

Christina Rossetti

My dear friend Emily is an American "snowbird." Shortly after Thanksgiving, in late November, Emily leaves her home in Philadelphia and heads south to the warmer climate in Florida. She spends the winter in the Sunshine State, and it is there that she shares Christmas with her family, when they are able to visit, or with other "snowbird" friends. Because Emily's children and grandchildren are scattered across the United States, Christmas together is not always possible and sending Christmas cards and packages was becoming a logistical nightmare. This problem was solved for the family by Emily's son, Chris. Several years ago, Chris proposed that, instead of family members trying to find gifts for each other, each family go to a church or family services group in their area and "adopt" an underprivileged family for Christmas. "We really don't need anything, Mom, and it seems like we could help some family that might not otherwise have a very happy Christmas."

Emily and the rest of the family members grabbed on to Chris's idea enthusiastically. Here's what Emily told me.

The Gift of Sharing

I called the pastor of our church and asked if he knew of any family that might need my help to make Christmas a little happier. He said that Florida Family Services had contacted him just that week looking for help for a single mother with three children. This mother was living on a very small allowance, raising her children and trying to complete her college education. Pastor Jim had a list of the children's ages, clothing sizes and, as well, suggestions for possible gifts for these needy youngsters.

I went home armed with my list and eager to begin my shopping for them. My neighbour, Della, heard of my plan and was anxious to contribute as well. We were shopping for two young girls, ages 13 and 11, and a 6 year old boy. We went to our area's largest department store and headed directly for the children's wear. Not really sure what young girls and boys these ages might like to wear, we enlisted the help of the sales staff as we made our choices. In the words of my great granddaughter, we were on a roll. We found everything, from underwear and socks to swimsuits, shorts, T-shirts and sweaters. We were having a wonderful time!

When we had found all that we felt they might need in clothing, we headed for other stores. We found paperbacks, books, games and gift certificates for theatres and fast-food restaurants. For mom, we found a Walkman (that she had requested) and a number of restaurant certificates. We were exhausted but completely elated as we headed home.

The next day we enlisted the help of neighbours to wrap the gifts, and one of our friends suggested that we should collect food for the family as well. As word spread, food began to show up at our doorstep in amazing amounts! Before it was time to deliver our gifts for the family, we had cases of food enough to last for many weeks.

Our neighbour, Wayne, who owned a large van, helped us deliver our goods to Pastor Jim at the church. He was overwhelmed when he saw what we had delivered.

Della and I returned home with a feeling of satisfaction that we had not felt for many years when Christmas shopping.

On Christmas morning I awoke with a wonderful feeling of happiness, knowing that I had helped to make a very special Christmas through the simple act of sharing.

My family felt the same way. All thought that this had been their best Christmas ever and even the youngest of the children had learned something of the joy of giving.

About a month later I received a letter from the family. It read, in part:

"Dear Kind Friends,

Thank you so much for all that you did for us at Christmas. When Pastor Jim arrived and began unloading your gifts and the boxes of food, I started to cry. We had so little in the refrigerator I wasn't sure what we would have for dinner. Thanks to your generosity, we will have wonderful dinners for many weeks to come.

Your gifts were extraordinary! My children had never had new clothes before; all of our shopping is done at the Thrift Stores.

I wish many blessings for you and your families and friends. I cannot find words to thank you for your generosity. I will remember you every day in my prayers and I hope that some day I will be able to do for others what you have done for us.

Bless you and thank you.

From:

A grateful family"

I don't remember when I enjoyed a happier Christmas. I hope that our family will continue this tradition for many years to come.

Although we do so much to get ready for a Christmas celebration, it wasn't so long ago that preparations were much more arduous and time-consuming.

In the days of the early settlers, chores were divided between men and women and each had specific jobs to tackle before Christmas Day.

Women's Pre-Christmas Tasks

- Clean the house
- Wash the tablecloths, rugs and curtains
- Press the best quilts
- Sew new clothes for every member of the family to wear at the Christmas parties
- Make jams and preserves
- Choose the best vegetables and fruits and store them separately to be used only at Christmas
- Prepare pies and cakes that can be made ahead of time
- Cook the sausage and roasts

- Make soups
- Make mincemeat for pies
- Prepare the plum pudding
- Set aside the best spices and herbs
- Pluck feathers from the goose, save for pillows
- Prepare a Christmas hamper for the minister and his family

Men's Pre-Christmas Tasks

- Cut firewood for the fireplace
- Bring the flour home from the mill
- Hunt or slaughter the animals and birds for roasting
- Prepare sausages, bacon and roasts to be cooked
- Repair, paint and varnish the sleighs
- Polish the Christmas sleigh bells
- Check the harness
- Air the bear, wolf and moose blankets for the sleighs
- Brush down the horses
- Run errands for the women
- Clear the road to the church
- Chop evergreens for decorations

When I read those lists, it makes me happy to be living in the present day.

Carols and Other Traditions

O come, o come, Emmanuel
And ransom captive Israel,
That mourns in lowly exile here
Until the Son of God appear.
Rejoice! Rejoice! Emmanuel
Shall come to thee, O Israel.

Traditional Carol

Christmas carols are some of the loveliest hymns ever sung in the church.

Opinions vary about the origins of the Christmas carol. Some believe the word "carol" comes from the Greek and Latin word "chorus," while others suggest the Latin word "corolla" (meaning crown, coronet or garland) is likely the root of the word. In ancient Greece where many circle dances were performed, the flute player who accompanied these dances was known as "choraules."

In medieval Britain and France the "carole" was a courtly dance song. Gradually the dance aspect lessened; carols with religious as well as secular texts began to appear, and carol singing became established in churches as well as homes and fair grounds.

The earliest surviving printed collection of English carols was published in 1521 by Wynkyn de Worde, an English printer of French origin.

In the 16th century, the changes brought about by the Reformation led to the decline of the carol. During the 17th century, religious carols almost completely disappeared.

In the 19th century, a number of collections of carols were published in England and America. This renewed interest led to new carols being composed and old ones being rediscovered.

Carols were very popular with music-loving Victorians. It became a Christmas Eve tradition to tour the streets singing such popular carols as "Angels from the Realms of Glory" or "Good King Wenceslas."

The affluent saw carolling as a means of doling out charity. Homeowners often paid the singers with coins or gifts of fruit or nuts. Carolers might also be invited in for a warming glass of punch or wassail and hot mince pie.

Many churches today have one or more special evenings of Christmas carol singing. Usually in the last few weeks before Christmas Day, a candlelight carol service is held, to which family members of all ages are welcomed to sing the many beloved traditional carols along with junior and senior choir members. In our area, the candlelight carol service is held the Friday evening before Christmas.

How beautiful it is to sing the haunting strains of "Silent Night" or the beloved children's carol, "Away in a Manger," as we stand amid the twinkling lights of our candles. It is a night that we all cherish.

Silent Night

Silent night! Holy night!
All is calm, all is bright.
Round yon Virgin Mother and Child
Holy Infant so tender and mild,
Sleep in heavenly peace,
Sleep in heavenly peace.

Silent night! Holy night!
Son of God, Love's pure light!
Radiant beams from thy holy face
With the dawn of redeeming grace.
Jesus, Lord at thy birth,
Jesus, Lord at thy birth.

R.W. Joseph Mohr

Away in a Manger

Away in a manger, no crib for a bed,
The little Lord Jesus lay down his sweet head.
The stars in the bright sky looked down where he lay,
The little lord Jesus asleep on the hay.

The cattle are lowing, the baby awakes,
But the little Lord Jesus no crying he makes.
I love thee, Lord Jesus; look down from the sky,
And stay by my side until morning is nigh.

Be near me, Lord Jesus, I ask thee to stay,
Close by me for ever, and love me, I pray.
Bless all the dear children in thy tender care,
And fit us for heaven, to live with thee there.

O Little Town of Bethlehem

O little town of Bethlehem
How still we see thee lie!
Above thy deep and dreamless sleep
The silent stars go by.
Yet in thy dark streets shineth
The everlasting Light;
The hopes and fears of all the years
Are met in thee tonight.

Phillip Brooks

It Came Upon the Midnight Clear

It came upon the midnight clear,
That glorious song of old,
From angels bending near the earth
To touch their harps with gold;
"Peace on the earth, goodwill to men
From heavens-all gracious King."
The world in solemn stillness lay,
To hear the angels sing.

Edmund H. Sears

After the carol service our family likes to enjoy a make-ahead dinner. One of our favourite meals is Spaghetti Pie with salad and garlic bread.

Spaghetti Pie

Spaghetti pies can be made a day ahead and refrigerated until baked.

3 cups cooked spaghetti (about 6 oz. / 185 g. dry)
2 tbsp. (30 mL) butter or margarine
2 eggs, beaten
⅓ cup (75 mL) Parmesan cheese, divided
1 cup (250 mL) cottage (or ricotta) cheese
1 tbsp. (15 mL) dried parsley flakes
1 lb. (500 g) lean ground beef (or sausage meat)
1 tbsp. (15 mL) Italian seasoning
1 can (680 mL) spaghetti sauce
½ cup (125 g) shredded mozzarella cheese

1. Cook spaghetti according to package directions. Drain. Return to pot. Add butter, eggs and Parmesan cheese. Mix well.
2. Spread spaghetti in a 9-inch (22.5-cm) greased pie plate, making a "crust."

3. In a bowl, mix cottage cheese and parsley flakes. Spread mixture evenly in the well of the pie crust.
4. Brown ground beef, and drain off fat. Mix Italian seasoning and spaghetti sauce into the beef and stir well, cooking until sauce bubbles. Spread beef mixture over the cottage cheese on the pie. (Be sure that the spaghetti is high enough on the edge that the cheese and beef mixtures are not going to overflow.)
5. Bake in a 350°F (180°C) oven for 25 minutes. Sprinkle with mozzarella cheese. Bake for 5 more minutes. Let stand for 5 minutes before serving. Cut into wedges.

Makes 6 servings (4 if heartier servings are wanted).

Mixed Green Salad

8 cups (2 L) mixed greens (or mesclun salad mix)
½ cup (125 mL) slivered red onion
½ cup (125 mL) toasted slivered almonds
½ cup (125 mL) toasted sunflower seeds

DRESSING
½ tsp. (2 mL) brown sugar
2 tbsp. (30 mL) red wine vinegar

2 tsp. (10 mL) dry mustard (you may substitute Dijon mustard)
1 tsp. (5 mL) minced garlic
⅓ cup (75 mL) olive oil
salt and pepper to taste

1. In a salad bowl combine salad greens, onions, nuts and seeds.
2. In a small bowl whisk together sugar, vinegar, mustard and garlic. Gradually whisk in oil. Pour over salad, and toss to coat. Add salt and pepper to taste.

Makes 6 servings.

Cheesy Garlic Bread

1 loaf French bread
⅓ cup (75 mL) butter
⅓ cup (75 mL) olive oil
3 tbsp. (45 mL) minced garlic
½ cup (125 mL) grated Parmesan cheese

1. Slice bread in half lengthwise.

2. In a small saucepan, melt butter over low heat. Add olive oil and garlic; stir well.
3. Place bread halves together on a baking sheet. Brush butter and garlic oil mixture evenly on the bread halves. Sprinkle grated Parmesan cheese on bread halves.
4. Broil bread about 6 inches (15 cm) from heat for about 2 minutes or until golden brown.

Serve warm.

Makes 8 to 10 servings.

Although I have always associated carolling with snow and visions of people in Victorian outfits, Christmas carols are sung in climates warm and cold around the world.

My good friends Marilyn and Larry Spicer, who live in Florida, enjoy carolling with neighbours in their condominium community each Christmas Eve. How much I enjoyed the photos they sent to me. It was unusual to see people wearing their summer attire standing in front of a lighted Santa's sleigh pulled by a red-nosed dolphin. The hundreds of miniature white lights decorating the palm trees completed a wonderful picture of warm-weather Christmas Eve.

I thank the unknown author for this poem, "Christmas in Florida," which reminds us of the first Christmas in Bethlehem, those many years ago.

The visitor sadly shook his head
As he baked in the tropical sun.
"Call this Christmas?" he said to me.
"Well, not where I come from.
Christmas needs snow and ice and cold,
And the sounds of sleigh bells ring.
And as for me I can't be sold
On weather that feels like spring."

We looked at him and then we smiled
As he scoffed at our awful plight.
And we felt pity and were not riled
'Cause he was so far from right.
For no snow fell on Bethlehem
On that night the first star shone.
There was no blizzard or howling gale
That swept with a shriek and a moan.

The breeze was soft and, what was more,
The night the Christ child came,
Hibiscus bloomed near that stable door
As Mary murmured His name.
Bougainvillea of violet hue,

Arched in a graceful bower;
Poinsettias wet with midnight dew
Enhanced that sacred hour.

The heavenly host in the starry sky
Proclaimed the birth of a king.
And rustling palms echoed the cry
As the whole world seemed to sing.
So we find here in the sun-drenched land
Untouched by ice and snow,
That the spirit of Christmas is at hand
And we feel God willed it so.

In Florida (and many other states and provinces along the sea coasts) a lovely Christmas tradition has developed. In the Yuletide season, boat owners decorate their yachts, large and small. While some of the yachts have simple decorations, perhaps a wreath on the bow, or lights on the rails, others have very elaborate light shows. Using extra generators for power, some yachtsmen have enormous displays on board that may include moving light arrangements with accompanying music. The local yacht clubs choose an evening when all of the decorated boats get together and travel along the coastline providing a wonderful show for the many hundreds of people who come to enjoy this very special occasion.

MARILYN

At the Treasure Island Yacht Club, the members host a "Parade Party." Anyone who wishes to view the boat parade from the wonderful vantage points afforded on the yacht club property need only bring a gift-wrapped child's toy to give to the collection for local needy children.

As well, members offer hot clam chowder, apple cider, hot dogs and Christmas cookies—all free of charge. It is usually an enormous crowd that enjoys this unique Christmas tradition.

Christmas is more than a gift-laden tree,
It is caring and sharing . . . unselfishly.

Author Unknown

The Wassail Song

Here we come a wassailing
Among the leaves so green,

Here we come a wand'ring
So fair to be seen:

Love and joy come to you,
And to you your wassail too,
And God bless you, and send you
A happy new year,
And God send you a happy new year.

Traditional Carol

The wassail bowl takes its name from the Anglo-Saxon term that means "Waes Hael," to be whole or hale. Originally an agricultural ritual, wassailing focused on apple orchards. Singing and humming as they went, the wassailers would carry a bowl filled with a special mixture of mulled cider made with apples and eggs that they would sprinkle on the roots of selected trees to ensure a good crop the following spring and summer.

As time passed, wassailing moved away from the orchards and into village streets, where it became a celebration of the Christmas holiday. Wassailers travelled from house to house, singing carols and sharing drinks from their bowl.

Wassail (Mulled Cider)—Christmas version

Wassail, or mulled cider, is still a popular drink to serve when carolers come calling.

24 whole cloves
1 orange
8 cups (2 L) apple cider
4 cups (1 L) cranberry juice
½ cup (125 mL) sugar
2 cinnamon sticks
1 tsp. (5 mL) Angostura bitters
24 whole allspice
1 cup (250 mL) dark rum (optional)

1. Press cloves into orange and put the orange in a heavy saucepan. Add cider, cranberry juice, sugar, cinnamon, bitters and allspice. Bring to a simmer, stirring until sugar dissolves. Reduce heat to low; cover and simmer 1½ hours.
2. Strain into punch bowl or crock pot and add rum if desired.

Makes 12 servings.

Whether it is carolers who come calling, or friends bringing best wishes for the season, it is nice to have a variety of snacks to serve at a moment's notice (or at least with a minimum of fuss or bother). These next recipes are handy when you need something to serve in a hurry.

Spicy Cheese Ball

1 lb. (500 g) old Cheddar cheese, shredded
4 oz. (125 g) cream cheese
¼ cup (50 mL) port, brandy or sherry
1 tbsp. (15 mL) crumbled dried tarragon, marjoram or oregano
pinch dried dill weed
2 drops Tabasco or your favourite hot sauce
¼ cup (50 mL) chopped fresh parsley

1. In a food processor, or in a bowl and using a fork, blend cheddar and cream cheeses, port, tarragon, dill weed and Tabasco until smooth. Roll into a ball.
2. Spread the chopped parsley on waxed paper; roll the cheese ball in parsley to coat. Wrap in plastic and refrigerate until chilled (cheese ball can be refrigerated for up to 2 weeks).

3. Serve with your favourite crackers or with a variety of fresh veggies.

Bacon Bagel Bites

This recipe appeals to my grandchildren but I also enjoy these little snacks.

1 pkg. frozen mini bagels, split and toasted (usually 10 per package)
½ cup (125 mL) chunky blue cheese dressing
6 slices bacon, cooked and crumbled
2 medium green onions, chopped

1. Spread each bagel half with about 1 tsp. (5 mL) dressing. Sprinkle with bacon and onion.
2. Arrange bagel halves on a baking sheet and broil about 6 inches (15 cm) from the heat for 2 minutes or until hot and bubbling. Serve immediately.

Makes 20 bagel bites.

Crab Dip with Toasted Almonds

This crab dip is sure to be a hit!

1 pkg. (8 oz./250 g) cream cheese
1 can (7 oz./200 g) crab meat, rinsed and drained
1 tbsp. (15 mL) parsley flakes
2 tbsp. (30 mL) mayonnaise
1 tsp. (5 mL) horseradish
1 tbsp. (15 mL) lemon juice
4 tbsp. (60 mL) sliced almonds, toasted

1. Put cream cheese in a bowl, and warm it in the microwave until softened. Stir in remaining ingredients, except almonds.
2. Spread the crab mixture evenly in an 8-inch (20-cm) round pie tin. Spread toasted almonds on the crab mix. Heat in a 350°F (180°C) oven until mixture is bubbling, 8 to 10 minutes. Serve hot with crackers, veggies or tortilla chips.

Stuffed Mushrooms

Stuffed mushrooms look good on all appetizer trays and there are any number of ways to stuff them.

To prepare mushrooms, wash and remove stems. As well, I like to cut out the inside of the mushroom until only the white of the cap remains.

SPINACH STUFFNG

1 pkg. (10 oz./310 g) frozen spinach soufflé, thawed
⅓ cup (75 mL) grated Parmesan cheese

1. Mix ingredients together and spoon into mushroom caps.
2. Heat in a 350°F (180°C) oven until heated through.

HAM AND CHEESE STUFFNG

1 pkg. (3 oz./90 g) cream cheese, softened
1½ tsp. (7 mL) butter (or margarine), softened
½ cup (125 mL) finely chopped ham
2 tbsp. (30 mL) bread crumbs
2 tbsp. (30 mL) finely chopped onion
½ tsp. Worcestershire sauce
salt to taste

Mix ingredients and spoon into mushroom caps. Heat in a 350°F (180°C) oven until mixture bubbles, 8 to 10 minutes.

Both stuffings will fill 10 to 15 small
or medium mushroom caps.

Christmas bestows upon mankind cheer and inspiration from the songs of carolers wending their way through the streets of cities and hamlets, to the hymns and homilies pouring from the pulpits and choir lofts of churches throughout the land. Let the bells and carols and the message of Christmas flow freely in praise of Him whose endowment to mankind is our heritage without end.

Lansing Christman

See amid the winter's snow,
Born for us on earth below;
See the tender lamb appears,
Promised from eternal years.

Hail, thou ever blessed morn;
Hail, redemption's happy dawn;

Sing through all Jerusalem
Christ is born in Bethlehem.

Teach, O teach us, Holy Child,
By thy face so meek and mild,
Teach us to resemble thee
In thy sweet humility.

Hail, thou ever blessed morn;
Hail, redemption's happy dawn;
Sing through all Jerusalem
Christ is born in Bethlehem.

Traditional Carol

Holiday Decorating

Midst balsam boughs and candlelight
With faces all aglow
We sit beside the cheery fire
And sing the songs we know.

Georgia B. Adams

Deck the halls with boughs of holly . . .

The custom of decorating homes with evergreens and candles for winter festivals predates Christmas. The Romans decorated their villas with greenery to celebrate Saturnalia, the winter festival. The evergreen was a symbol of eternal life because it was able to survive the winter. Candles have been lighting holy days since the beginning of recorded time, and today Christmas candles symbolize Christ, the Light of the World.

European tribes often hung circles of greenery on their doors to welcome friends to their homes. The circle represented the continuous circle of life. Anglo-Saxons believed that mistletoe would protect houses against witchcraft, while ensuring fertility for those living in the home. The Christmas wreath, traditionally made from evergreen boughs, is thought to have originated as a symbol of Christ's crown of thorns.

Along with evergreens, many other plants are considered to be traditional Christmas favourites. As well as holly and ivy, such flowering plants as amaryllis, azalea, Christmas cactus and paperwhites are pretty ways of dressing up the home for the holiday season. The poinsettia, another of the lovely Christmas plants, has a most interesting story attached to it. A lovely legend from Mexico tells of Pablo, a poor young Mexican boy who picked a branch of the plant to bring to Jesus at the shrine of the nativity. When Pablo placed his branch on the altar, the leaves miraculously turned brilliant red and his gift was transformed into a beautiful flower.

The poinsettia plant has tiny flowers surrounded by large flower-like upper leaves that turn a brilliant red (or, less commonly, pink or white). With the striking contrast between the red and green leaves, the poinsettia rivals the holly as one of the most popular Christmas plants.

The poinsettia, native to Mexico, was first brought to the United States in 1828 by Joel Roberts Poinsett, a botanist and the first American ambassador to Mexico. By the early 1830s, the plant was being grown in Charleston, North Carolina (Poinsett's home), and by other of his botanist friends in Philadelphia. By the early 1900s, flower growers in California had developed the potted Christmas poinsettia.

It's a tradition in our family that my son-in-law, Bruce, brings his wife, Marg, and me the first poinsettia plant of the season, usually in late November. Many of my friends, knowing of my love for these plants, also send along one or two to each of us with their greetings for the season. By Christmas day, our home resembles a florist's shop and this is just how we love to see it.

There are a number of ways to decorate both inside and out using greenery and variety of plants. The following suggestions are just a few of my favourites.

Christmas in a Summer Pot

At Christmas Marg and I get out several pots that we use for our summer plants. These summer pots can be made to look very seasonal with a minimum of effort.

MATERIALS

Pots of various sizes
A variety of evergreen boughs
Eucalyptus branches
Baby's breath
Seasonal ribbons

- Arrange the evergreen boughs, eucalyptus branches and baby's breath in the pots. Tie a ribbon around each pot and make a bow.
- Larger pots look nice on coffee tables or in the front hall. Smaller pots look attractive on window sills, particularly if you put candles between the pots.
- Marg also likes to use a number of different size pots in a grouping on the kitchen table. Tapers arranged between the pots create a wonderful centrepiece.

Decorating with Baskets

Wicker baskets are readily available in department stores and many grocery stores.

MATERIALS

Wicker baskets
Potted mums or poinsettia plants to fit baskets
Evergreen boughs
Pine cones
Gold or silver glitter spray
Miniature Christmas lights (set of 25)

1. Place a mum or poinsettia plant in each basket. Arrange evergreen boughs and pine cones in the basket.
2. Spray plants with glitter spray. When dry, place basket near an electrical outlet (or use an extension cord) and weave the lights among the plants. When they are turned on, a shimmering effect is achieved as the lights glint off thc glitter.

Basket Wreath

MATERIALS

1 piece of chicken wire (12" × 16"/30 × 40 cm)
1 grapevine wreath 16" (40 cm) in diameter
Small plastic margarine container
Grapevines (or other pliable branches)
Floral wire
Strips of birch bark
Spanish moss
Evergreen branches
Dried baby's breath
Glue gun
Floral foam
1½ yards (135 cm) wired ribbon 2" (5 cm) wide
3 or 4 artificial red berry picks
5 or 6 pinecones

1. Lay chicken wire over the bottom half of the wreath. Bend the edges around the vines so they are held in place at the back of the wreath.
2. Set the plastic container on the chicken wire inside the wreath. Loosely weave the grapevines over the container from side to side and in and out of the wreath at each side, so the container is held

securely in place and is well hidden. Reinforce with floral wire if necessary. Weave birch bark strips around the container and fill any small gaps with moss. Use the glue gun to secure floral foam into the bottom of the plastic container.

3. Twist a length of vine into a bow. Secure it with wire. Wire and glue the vine bow to the top of the wreath slightly off centre. Insert evergreen branches and baby's breath into the floral foam.
4. Make one large bow and one smaller bow from the wired ribbon. Wire and glue the large bow to the chicken wire basket, just off centre, and the smaller bow on to the vine bow. Arrange the tails of both bows and glue them in place.
5. Wire and glue berries and pine cones in place on the wreath.

Miniature Trees

MATERIALS

Dried lemon leaves (available at most florists)
Foam cones
Glue gun
Tiny wooden star (available at most craft stores)

1. Air-dry the lemon leaves (the leaves are thick and leathery and will curl into interesting shapes).
2. Starting at the bottom of the cone, glue the leaves to the cone to look like tree branches.
3. Glue the star to the top and set the "tree" on any table.

Ice Wreaths

For people living in very cold climates, ice wreaths are a delightful way to decorate outdoors. Made with fresh holly, these wreaths can be hung from tree branches in your garden. As long as the temperature remains below freezing, you'll have a lovely reminder of the Christmas season.

MATERIALS

Round mould for jellies
Fresh holly branches with berries
Heavy-duty ribbon
Nail or sturdy hook

1. Fill the mould about half full with water and freeze. This is the base of the wreath. Arrange holly over top, add water to fill mould and freeze solid.

2. Place bottom of mould in warm water; the wreath will pop out. Hang wreath from a nail or hook with heavy-duty ribbon.

There are many easy ways to add Christmas touches all through your home—use cedar or pine boughs with giant pine cones and red ribbon to make garlands for doorways, window sills and stair railings.

Wooden bowls filled with nuts, pine cones and small pine branches and cinnamon sticks look lovely on side tables or in hallways.

If you have a large tall vase or perhaps an umbrella stand, you can make a very pretty decoration. Spray a number of large twigs with white paint. Arrange the twigs in the vase with some pine branches. Add some miniature twinkle lights and tiny red bows and you have a most attractive decoration for your front hall.

My Gift

What do I want for Christmas?
Lord, set one bright star apart
And let me lift to it this night
An awed and childlike heart.

Author Unknown

Let every pudding burst with plums,
And every tree bear dolls and drums,
In the week when Christmas comes.

Eleanor Farjeon

Candles have been a part of Christmas tradition for a very long time. For two thousand years, Europeans have lit candles in their churches and homes to welcome the Christ Child, the Light of the World. Today people still use candles as decorative touches, using them on mantlepieces, in chandeliers and as table centrepieces, to mention just a few.

Candles today come in an amazing variety of shapes and sizes and colours. At Christmas, the most common colours for candles are white, red or green.

Add a decorator's touch to your candle displays by applying gold leaf to the candles' surface, a process known as "gilding." You can find gold leaf in craft shops, and you'll discover that this project is easy to complete in very little time. These beautiful candles also make lovely gifts.

Gilded Candles

MATERIALS

Brown craft paper (for the work surface)
Butter knife with a blade longer than 5½" (13.75 cm)
1 book of gold composition leaf (usually sold in a book of 25 square sheets about 5½" (13.75 cm) square)
Pillar candles, wrapped in cellophane, as they already have an adhesive surface
Cotton balls

1. Lay the craft paper on a clean work surface. Dampen the butter knife slightly with your breath, then use the knife to lift a sheet of gold leaf onto the kraft paper.
2. Unwrap the cellophane wrapper from the candle, touching exposed surfaces as little as possible.

There are two ways to affix the gold leaf to the candles.

(i) With completely dry fingertips, break the sheet of gold leaf into pieces by pulling it apart. The leaf is fragile and will break quite easily into irregular shapes and sizes. Press pieces of the gold leaf onto the candles, using your fingertips.

(ii) For more complete candle coverage, hold the candle top and bottom, then position it diagonally on the edge of the leaf and roll the candle across the sheet so the gold adheres to the candle.
Repeat (for both i and ii), with additional sheets of gold leaf until the surface is gilded as desired. Leaving gaps will give your candles an antique look or you can fill the gaps with torn pieces.

3. Rub a cotton ball over the surface to polish the leaf to a shiny finish. Any excess flakes of gold leaf can also be brushed off with a cotton ball.

Note: It's important to work with metal leaf in a dust- and wind-free area, as leaf is light and may blow away.

You can also use metal leaf on such items as glass Christmas ball, decorative wooden boxes, wicker baskets or plastic fruit. With these items, the trick is that you must use size (a special glue) in order for the leaf to adhere to the surface. When gilding on these items is complete, seal using a water-based satin sealer.

Lo! The Light!

Above the manger stood a star,
A star all wondrous white;

And all about His lowly bed
There welled a flood of light.

It bathed the stable in its glow,
It shone 'round Mary's head;
And on the kneeling shepherds' cloaks
Its radiant beams were shed.

Star of the world! Through time and space,
It flames in glory bright
To make man's pathway through the years
A pilgrimage of light.

It shines for us—that light still shines!
No cloud can dim its spark;
Its radiance blossoms bright with joy,
A beacon of the dark.

The path leads on, the path leads up;
We walk it mile by mile,
And lo! The light His love has lit
Grows brighter all the while.

Oh never doubt it shines for you,
Though skies seem dark and low—
Keep looking up, keep lifted up,
Somewhere a star will show.

Let not your heart be trouble filled,
The darkest night must clear,
And life be glad and life be sweet,
For lo! The light is here!

Elizabeth Landeweer

Flea markets, thrift shops and garage sales are wonderful places to look for candle holders. Marg and I have a great many holders in all shapes and sizes that we use in the Yuletide season. As well, unusual containers such as terra cotta pots, old wooden bobbins, planters, urns or glass jars and bottles make fine holders for candles large and small.

Candlelight gives a warm glow to any room, including the kitchen. An easy trick is to use a six-cup muffin tin. Cut red votive candles in half horizontally, and place the top half in the centre of each muffin cup. Discard the metal base and remaining wick piece. Melt the remaining wax and pour it around each candle. Set the muffin tin on a cloth Christmas napkin and surround it with several pine boughs. It's guaranteed to brighten any corner of your kitchen.

Another simple but very attractive project uses glass candle votives, bay leaves, holly berries and raffia.

With a hot glue gun, attach bay leaves to the sides of the glass. Add a raffia bow and some holly berries and a candle and you'll have a decoration or hostess gift that was easy to make but very effective.

If you have a wide window ledge, you can make your window look lovely from inside and out. Pair a half-dozen pillar candles of various heights with glass vases that are tall enough to extend above the candle's flame. Pour a small amount of coarse salt into each vase and set the candle in the salt. Surround the vases with holly branches.

My daughter Julia has an interesting way to decorate with floating candles. She fills a number of large glass bowls with water and, in the water, she places fresh cut flowers from which she has cut the stems. She then places floating candles among the flowers to create a beautiful reflecting pool. Setting the bowls on silver trays or mirrors adds an even more elegant touch to this eye-appealing display.

On a very special occasion, Julia has even floated flowers and candles in her bathtub—an attractive surprise for guests using the facilities.

Oftentimes simple is best. You can create a delightful glow by using tea-light candles. They're inexpensive to buy in bags of 100 and can be placed in mismatched wine glasses and juice glasses and used on kitchen or dining-room tables, fireplace mantles, or anywhere you can find a flat surface.

My granddaughter Phyllis often buys bags of fresh or

frozen cranberries that she uses to half-fill Mason jars. She ties raffia bows around the neck and inserts a tall white candle into the cranberries. (Be sure that the candle is stable so it will not burn the raffia as the candle wax melts.)

Luminarias

A most interesting use of candles, known as "luminarias," began as a Spanish Christmas custom and has found its way to North America. These small lantern-type lights have, for centuries, been the symbolic way to light the arrival of the Blessed Babe on Christmas Eve.

In Spain, the first luminarias were bonfires set to light the way for the Christ Child. With the advent of coloured wrapping paper, people found it easier to use paper lanterns rather than the traditional bonfires. It became customary to string lanterns through the trees or hang them from wires around the house.

As more and more Spanish people emigrated to Mexico, they brought the custom with them and it gradually spread into the southwestern United States, particularly New Mexico and Texas. In the early 1800s, Yankee traders coming down the Santa Fe Trail brought brown paper bags with them. Somehow it was decided that these small bags could be used for the luminaries and they have been used for the "Little Lights of Christmas" ever since.

Luminarias are easy to make. You need large brown paper grocery bags (those that have a flat bottom), sand and candles. The luminaria is made in three easy steps.

1. Fold down a 2-inch (5 cm) cuff at the top of the bag.
2. Fill the bottom of the bag with 3 or 4 inches (7.5 or 10 cm) of sand.
3. Place the candle securely in the centre of the sand.

Luminarias are an energy-saving way to decorate your driveway, walkways, sidewalks or porch.

There is no danger of fire, as the candle is in the centre of the bag, away from the side. When the candle has burned down, it will be extinguished by the sand. However, the luminarias should be placed carefully so as to avoid being near flammable materials, pedestrian traffic, strong winds, etc.

On Christmas Eve in New Mexico, entire villages are lit up using only luminarias. Through December, residents make hundreds of the "lanterns," and on Christmas Eve all other lights in the town are turned off. So spectacular is the sight that many thousands of people travel to New Mexico just to see this dazzling display.

Making luminarias is a fun project for grandchildren. My great-grandchildren, Bethany and Michael, like to decorate the paper bags with crayon pictures or with cutouts from old Christmas cards that they glue on to the bags. The "Little Lights of Christmas" make a welcoming sight as the family returns from the evening church service.

It's Christmas

Candles lighted in a row,
Casting shadows as they glow.
Holly, pine and mistletoe,
On the lawn new-fallen snow.

Stockings bulging, how they strain—
By the mantel once again.
Eager faces breathless pause—
Speechless wonders of Santa Claus.

Children's laughter, oh what joy
For each small girl and each small boy
Surprise and rapture in each eye—
Have you guessed the reason why?

It's Christmas!

Author Unknown

Family Traditions

What I'd like to have for Christmas
I can tell you in a minute.
The family all around me,
And the home with laughter in it.

Edgar A. Guest

Pierre Berton, the Canadian journalist, once said, "To me, ritual is the glue that keeps society together. Family rituals, like vacations with the whole family, are important things. To get a sense of community; that is what gives people peace of mind and security."

The Christmas season offers a marvellous opportunity to establish traditions that the family will remember and treasure for many years. Sometimes the things our children remember best from childhood are the simple rituals. Hanging the stockings on Christmas Eve, baking shortbread cookies and making gingerbread houses can make beautiful memories when they are repeated year after year.

Our family has established a number of early "not to be missed" events that your families may also enjoy during the holiday season.

"Christmas Movie Night" (or nights, as there are so many outstanding seasonal films) is a particular favourite. Early in December, my grandson Fred or his wife, June, will call and say, "Saturday is movie night—hope you can come." Many family members have been known to cancel other plans so as to not miss the evening.

My favourite of the old films is the 1951 version of Charles Dickens' *A Christmas Carol*. Alistair Sims was critically acclaimed for his brilliant portrayal of Mr. Scrooge, and even the youngest in the family love this most famous of Christmas films.

It's a Wonderful Life, the 1946 film starring Jimmy Stewart and Donna Reed, is based on the short story "The Greatest Gift" by Philip Van Doren Stern. George Bailey, played by Jimmy Stewart, is the manager of a small savings and loan company in a small American town. When he questions his worth in this world, an angel appears to save him and raise his Christmas spirits.

The 1947 version of *Miracle on 34th Street* and the more recent *The Grinch Who Stole Christmas*, appeal especially to the youngsters in the families, and I could watch *Hol-*

iday Inn over and over again, if only to hear Bing Crosby's immortal crooning of "White Christmas."

When we all get together for these movies, we like to have a simple meal such as lasagna with salad, or perhaps pizza, which we order in. Of course no movie night is complete without enormous bags of popcorn and hot chocolate with marshmallows. The younger children put on their pyjamas and slippers and we spread sleeping bags and pillows on the floor for added comfort. If the little ones fall asleep, it's easy to transport them to the car for the ride home.

A Victorian Christmas celebration was never complete without games. One strange game called Snapdragon was very popular. A dish of brandy was placed on the floor and set aflame. Handfuls of currants were tossed into the bowl and the object of the game was to grab a burning currant out of the fire—in your mouth—and in doing so, extinguish it.

Happily, many other games were far less dangerous; Hide and Seek, Bob Apple and Blind Man's Bluff are still familiar today. Charades was also a popular pastime.

In our family we play Christmas Scrabble. On Christmas afternoon the Scrabble board comes out, and anyone not directly involved in working on the dinner takes a turn in challenging for the highest score. In our house, we allow the players to score double points for using any words that pertain to Christmas. Scores are actually kept from year to year, and all participants are hoping to catch my great-grandson Justin's score—he has held top honours for three years running.

Playing Scrabble may seem like a simple thing, but it is a tradition that is enjoyed by young and old alike.

For several years now, our family has followed the instructions given in the December issue of the *Good Housekeeping* magazine to replicate prize-winning gingerbread houses selected from entries across North America. Those of us in the "older generation" work together on the house that will be the centrepiece, but we also provide ingredients for the children to make their own miniature houses.

Although we call them "gingerbread" houses, they are really cookie houses. Grandchildren and great-grandchildren look forward to the activity during the holiday season every year. This is also an activity that keeps youngsters occupied for hours, particularly if you suggest that they make a town with a variety of decorated homes.

Cookie House

INGREDIENTS

Assorted large crackers and cookies (Use varieties such as square graham wafers, Social Teas, or Wasa Crisps, for building and try sugar wafers, scalloped butter cookies or chocolate wafers for decorating)

1 batch of Thick Royal Icing (see below) or one tub of ready-to-use ornamental frosting (*not* ready-to-use regular frosting), usually available wherever cake decorating equipment is sold

Assorted decorations, including colourful candies, Smarties or M&M's, gum drops, miniature candy canes, coloured mini-Chiclets and tiny cinnamon hearts

THICK ROYAL ICING

4 cups (1 L) confectioner's sugar

2 egg whites

1½ tsp. (7 mL) fresh lemon juice, strained

1. Using a wooden spoon, stir about half the sugar into the egg whites. Add the lemon juice and beat the mixture with a wooden spoon until it is thoroughly blended.
2. Add the remaining sugar a little at a time, beating well after each addition. Continue to beat for 15 minutes or until the mixture is smooth and creamy.

The icing can be used immediately or kept for about 30 minutes if covered with a damp cloth. If kept longer, the icing will begin to set.

Assemble houses or other structures using large crackers or cookies, attaching each piece with Royal Icing. Spread the icing on the edges of the cookies to be joined and hold together for a few minutes until set (if young children are involved, you might choose to assemble a few houses before they arrive and let them do the decorating only).

Decorate as desired. Decorations can be easily attached with Royal Icing. Here are a few ideas.

Make a log cabin by icing the outer walls and attaching pretzel sticks.

Make a church steeple with an iced sugar wafer and a pretzel cross. Trim wafers for the doors of the church and make stained glass windows by cutting small pieces from gum drops.

Chocolate wafers make a great roof. Spread icing generously on the roof and then overlap the wafers slightly, starting at the bottom.

Use unfilled ice-cream cones to make castle turrets and candy canes to make lampposts. Candy canes can also make great sleigh runners for Santa's sleigh. The sleigh can be made from wafers.

Pine cones with dabs of frosting and tiny cinnamon hearts can serve as decorated trees for your village.

With imagination, there is no end to the enjoyment that children can have with this activity. Even teenagers who at first offer just to help the little ones usually wind up making their own house or village.

My great-grandchildren, Justin and Jenny, who are presently away at university, have told me that they can hardly wait to get home and start on the gingerbread houses. In spite of their "mature" age, they look forward to this yearly activity with unbridled enthusiasm.

It's the little things that count,
The things of every day;
Just the simple things that we can do,

The kind words we can say.
The little things like a friendly smile
For those who may be sad.
The clasp of a hand or a kindly deed
To help make someone glad.
A knock on the door of lonely homes,
Or flowers bright and gay.
For someone to whom you might bring cheer
With just a small bouquet.
Just the little greetings here and there
On which so much depends.
The little pleasures that all can share
The joy of making friends.

This little poem is an excellent reminder to us during the holiday season. For many people, Christmas is not the happiest time of the year. For shut-ins or friends living in nursing homes, it is a time when they may feel forgotten. It is important to make time in our busy schedules to stop in with a card or perhaps a poinsettia with a Christmas candle. "It's the little things in life that count." Make someone else's day a little happier and you are sure to brighten your own.

Children can learn a wonderful lesson of caring and sharing at this time of year. Visits to a nursing home to sing carols or to take gifts of homemade cookies allow children to know that they, too, may bring a little joy into the lives of others—not just their own homes, but in the community in which they live. These kind gestures easily become rituals that can be carried into their lives as adults and then passed on to succeeding generations.

These Are Needed

It takes much more than candle light
To make a Christmas glow,
Or trees with tinsel shining bright,
Or ice, or glittering snow.

It takes a smile, a hand clasped tight,
And love, and heartfelt prayer,
Kind thoughts, good deeds, and wrongs made right,
All these can prove we care.

Let's make this Christmas season bright
And glowing as of old,
When shone that first and glorious light—
A star as bright as gold.

Let's smile and help the world be gay,
Extend a friendly hand,
And make the world more bright this day,
This is the way God planned.

Author Unknown

Another favourite activity in our family is our annual "light night." We bundle the youngest children into their pyjamas, wrap them in blankets and tuck them into the car. We then drive through the neighbourhood to see as many lights and decorations as we can.

Christmas

Every time a hand reaches out
To help another,
That is Christmas.

Every time someone puts anger aside
And strives for understanding,
That is Christmas.

Every time people forget their differences
And realize their love for each other,
That is Christmas.

May this Christmas bring us
Closer to the spirit of human understanding,
Closer to the blessing of peace.

Author Unknown

Christmas Gifts

People say that Christmas today is too commercialized. But I have never found it that way. If you spend money to give people joy, you are not being commercial. It is only when you feel obliged to do something about Christmas that the spirit is spoiled.

Eleanor Roosevelt

I wrote earlier in the book about gifts to give from the kitchen, but now I'd like to offer a few ideas that might be helpful when you are looking for that "perfect" present.

At this time of year many people wonder what to buy for elderly relatives. My friends and I have talked together and we've come up with a few suggestions that are our favourites. Here are some of them. . . .

- A pre-paid phone card. Many of us would like to keep in touch with far-off friends and long-distance calling is expensive.
- Restaurant gift certificates. For those of us on a

fixed budget, eating out is an almost impossible luxury.

- Books on tapes. As our old eyes get weaker, it's wonderful to enjoy the printed word with our ears.
- A "Meal of the Week" gift. My daughter Mary started this a number of years ago. She chooses one day in the week and she delivers a full dinner for two. I can invite a girlfriend over and have absolutely no preparation work to do. My guest and I have a nice visit while we enjoy a delightful dinner. You younger folks may not realize what a wonderful present this is, but believe me when I tell you that it's a gift I enjoy more with each passing year.
- Your time. Nothing is a finer gift than time spent in your presence.

The most vivid memories of Christmas past are usually not of the gifts received or given, but of the spirit of love, the special warmth of Christmas worship, the cherished little habits of the home.

Lois Rand

While this sentiment is absolutely true, there are certain occasions when the gift is so special that it is cherished and remembered for a lifetime. This next story comes from my friend Virginia Smith and it gladdens my heart each time I think of it.

A Gift of Life

It was mid-November when Ginny noticed that her son Cody was just not his usual self. A normally high-energy youngster, he was sleeping much more than he usually did, seemed listless and was extremely pale.

Ginny took her young son to the doctor and it was thought he might have mononucleosis. That test came back negative, but Cody's condition continued to deteriorate. The doctor wanted to see Cody again to do an ultrasound and a C.B.C. (complete blood count) test.

Ginny was at work on December 6 when she got the call from the doctor. An ambulance was on the way to her home; she needed to get there immediately and was to accompany Cody on the trip from Gravenhurst, Ontario, to the Hospital for Sick Children in Toronto. On the ride to Toronto, Ginny had to digest the news that her five-year-old son had leukemia.

Upon her arrival at Sick Kids, as this world-renowned hospital is known, Cody's blood had virtually no platelets. He was given a platelet transfusion but before it could take effect, he began having seizures and was transferred to the Intensive Care Unit. Cody was desperately ill.

During the next few days, Ginny never left the hospital. A single mom, Ginny was in a new relationship with Jim, and it was he who brought Cody's sister, Taylor, to the hospital. There, Ginny's parents met them and took Taylor to their home so that Jim could be with Ginny and Cody.

The medical assault on Cody's leukemia began immediately. His blood was removed and filtered and chemotherapy begun as the doctors attempted to get Cody into remission.

As the days marched on toward Christmas, the townspeople of Gravenhurst rallied around the young family. Gifts were collected and delivered to the hospital. Money was donated to help pay the expenses, as Ginny was off work and staying at the nursing students' residence across from the hospital. While less expensive than a motel, it was still more than Ginny could afford.

On Christmas day, the family made every effort to have a happy time together. They decorated a small tree and opened the gifts that had been so generously provided by the hometown folks. Ginny's parents brought turkey and it was as close to a normal Christmas as was possible.

On Boxing Day, Cody went back into the I.C.U. where he remained until January 7. He gradually responded to treatment and the good news was that

Cody was in remission. . . . The bad news was that he would need a bone marrow transplant if he was to have any hope of a cure.

As Cody took his daily chemo treatments, the call went out to relatives in the search to find a possible donor match.

At the end of February, it was determined that Taylor was an exact match and the transplant date was set for April 16.

The transplant went so well that instead of having to stay in the hospital until June, Cody went home early—in time for Mother's Day in May.

On April 16, 2003, Cody was five years clear of leukemia and five seems to be the magic number that doctors use to indicate that a person has been cured of cancer.

Although Taylor's gift can't be considered a "Christmas present," she has given her brother the gift of many Christmases to come—a gift whose value is beyond measure!

Last Minute Gift Suggestions

To your enemy, forgiveness.
To an opponent, tolerance.
To a friend, your heart.
To every child, a good example.

To all, charity.
To yourself, respect.

For many of us senior citizens living on a fixed income, finding inexpensive but appropriate Christmas gifts can sometimes be a difficult task.

My dear friend Alice solved her problem in a way that I think is wonderful. She explained, "You know, Edna, when James and I were married we were very fortunate. We both came from families that were well to do and over the years we were given rather extravagant gifts. We had several sets of elegant china, crystal and silver, dozens of silver candle holders and a collection of Royal Doulton figurines.

"A few years ago, I decided to give some of my gifts to my family while I am alive, instead of leaving them in my will. I don't have an enormous income, but I do have lovely things that I rarely use. I decided that I would much rather see them used by my children or grandchildren when I can enjoy the pleasure that these gifts bring to them."

George and I had a lovely collection of hand bells that we had found on our many trips from one coast of Canada to the other. Over the years, I have given these bells to my daughters and their families and I love to see that they are being enjoyed as much in their new homes as they were when George and I displayed them in the manses of our parishes.

If you are stuck for a gift idea, try looking in your own home.

Another gift to treasure is one that is often overlooked: the family portrait. I like how Nancy Skarmeas explained it. "As precious as a beautiful family photograph is in the present, it becomes only more so with the passage of time. As memories fade, as children grow, as we all age and change and one generation replaces another, photographs keep us connected."

Many department stores offer special values on Christmas portraits but even amateur photos taken at a family gathering sometimes give the most accurate glimpse of the joy of the family being together.

Picture frames can be found in a variety of places, from dollar stores, to antique shops or second-hand and thrift shops. Often a coat of paint will give new life to old frames and make your photograph a gift to be cherished for generations.

Gifts

What shall we give the children?
Christmas is almost here . . .
Toys and games and playthings,
As we do every year?

Yes, for the magic of toyland
Is part of the Yuletide lore
To gladden the heart of childhood
But I shall give something more.

I shall give them more patience,
A more sympathetic ear,
A little more time for laughter,
Or to tenderly dry a tear.

I shall take the time to teach them
The joy of doing some task.
I'll try to find time to answer
More of the questions they ask.

Time to read books together,
And to take long walks in the sun. . .
Time for bedtime story
After the day is done.

I shall give these to my children,
Weaving a closer tie . . .
Knitting our lives together
With gifts that money can't buy

Isla Paschal Richardson

Gift Wrap

Somehow not only for Christmas
But all the long year through,
The joy that you give to others
Is the joy that comes back to you.
John Greenleaf Whittier

When you have finally found all the gifts you may need, it's time to start that very time-consuming job—wrapping the presents. With just a little ingenuity the ordinary becomes extraordinary and family and friends will remember your gift for a very long time to come.

One of the best gift containers is a wicker basket. Baskets are readily available in all sizes and shapes at most second-hand or thrift stores. Marg and I like to collect baskets all year long so that by Christmas we have a wide variety. We buy cans of spray paint in red, white, green, silver and gold and tissue paper in the same colours.

We usually spray paint the baskets early in December so they have lots of time to dry (and any odour of paint is gone). We wrap presents in tissue, either to match or contrast with the colour of the basket. A large bow on the handle and your gift is ready to go.

A basket is particularly nice to use if you are giving a number of small gifts to one person. Coloured cellophane wrapped around the basket will ensure that no part of your gift falls out. A bow or sprig of fresh holly completes the look.

You can wrap gifts for use in the kitchen in colourful tea towels. I often wrap decorative hand soaps in a terry washcloth and tie them with ribbon.

Any gift will take on a special look when sprigs of fresh holly or mistletoe are tied into the ribbon. Gold- or silver-sprayed pine cones also add a decorative touch to any paper-wrapped gift.

My daughter Marg likes to buy a number of Christmas tree balls that have the year inscribed on them. She puts one on each family member's gift and this gives them a memento to add to the tree in the following years.

Children enjoy helping with gift wrapping. Brown and white paper bags are fun for kids to decorate with stickers, markers, paint or glue and glitter. You may simply slip the gifts, along with tissue paper, into the bags. Many stores use plain coloured boxes at Christmas time and you need only to add a bright ribbon to look festive.

As wrapping gifts can be very time-consuming, experts suggest making it a team effort. If one person folds the paper, another can put on the tape, another adds ribbon or other decoration and someone else adds the gift tags. If there aren't this many people in your family, gift wrapping offers a great opportunity to have friends come over (bringing their gifts with them as well), and everyone will be happy to enjoy good company while completing this important Christmas chore.

If your family feels as we do, a wrapping party will certainly need a variety of delicious snacks. This tasty Hot Artichoke Dip is something that fills the bill.

Hot Artichoke Dip

This dip may be refrigerated (covered) up to 2 days. Reheat before serving.

1 tsp. (5 mL) minced garlic
1 can (14 oz. / 440 g) artichoke hearts (or bottoms), drained
1 cup (250 mL) grated Parmesan cheese
8 oz. (250 g) cream cheese at room temperature
½ cup (125 mL) mayonnaise

½ tsp. (2 mL) dried dill
½ tsp. (2 mL) parsley flakes

1. Using either a food processor or a blender, mix together the garlic and artichokes until puréed. Add the Parmesan cheese, cream cheese, mayonnaise and dill, and blend until smooth.
2. Transfer the mixture to a saucepan and cook over low heat, stirring until heated through. Serve with a variety of vegetables or nacho chips.

Sourdough Bread Bowl, with Brie

This is another family favourite.

1 sourdough bread loaf (round)
olive oil—enough to brush on the outside of the bread loaf
1 lb. (500 g) brie (white rind removed)
¼ to ½ cup (65 to 125 mL) sliced almonds

1. Pre heat the oven to 325°F (180°C). Spread sliced almonds on a cookie sheet and bake in the oven until toasted. Remove and set aside.

2. Slice the top off the round bread loaf and remove the white of the bread to leave a "bowl."
3. Break the removed portion of the bread into bite-sized pieces. Brush olive oil on the outside of the bread bowl and set the bowl on an ungreased cookie sheet. Spread the bite-sized pieces on the same cookie sheet and bake in a preheated oven until the bowl is hot to the touch and the bread bites are lightly toasted.
4. While the bread is toasting, cut the cheese into small chunks (about 1"/2.5 cm squares) and place in a microwaveable bowl. Heat on medium setting in the microwave oven for about 6 minutes, removing about every 30 seconds to stir as the cheese melts. Remove from microwave when the cheese is completely melted. Pour the cheese into the heated bread bowl and cover the cheese with the toasted almonds.
5. Place the bread bowl on a large serving platter and surround it with the bite-sized pieces of bread. Provide small knives or spoons for scooping out the cheese. Be sure to have a sharp knife available as well, as people will devour the bowl.

Pepperoni Pizza Dip

My great-grandchildren are pizza lovers so this recipe really appeals to them.

½ cup (125 mL) sour cream
1 pkg. (8 oz./250 g) cream cheese, softened
1 tsp. (5 mL) Italian seasoning
½ cup (125 mL) pizza sauce
½ cup (125 mL) pepperoni, chopped
¼ cup (50 mL) green onions, chopped
½ cup (125 mL) mozzarella cheese, shredded
corn chips, nacho chips or crisp bread sticks

1. Preheat oven to 350°F (180°C). In a small bowl, beat sour cream, cream cheese and Italian seasoning on medium speed until smooth (1 to 2 minutes). Spread evenly in a 9-inch (22.5-cm) pie pan.
2. Spread the pizza sauce over the mixture. Top with pepperoni and green onions. Bake for 10–12 minutes or until heated through.
3. Sprinkle the mozzarella cheese on top and continue baking for 4 to 5 minutes until the cheese has melted. Serve with a variety of chips or bread sticks.

Santa Claus

"Chubby and plump—a right jolly old elf," Santa Claus is a traditional part of Christmas folklore. The origin of Santa Claus can be traced back to St. Nicholas, a generous bishop in fourth-century Turkey who was said to perform kind deeds and bring gifts to the needy. Over time, St. Nicholas evolved into a magical figure who could fly (as witches did) and use chimneys as doors (like the Norse gods).

Santa's physical image has changed over the years. For hundreds of years St. Nicholas was imagined to be tall and thin. However, in "A Visit from St. Nicholas," a poem written in 1822 by Clement C. Moore, the saint is pictured as a round figure wearing a fur parka and riding in a sleigh pulled by eight reindeer.

An 1863 drawing by American political cartoonist Thomas Nast depicts Santa Claus as a big, red-faced, white-bearded, jolly man wearing sprigs of mistletoe and holly on his hat. Nast's famous 1866 drawing, "Santa Claus and His Works," showing Santa in his workshop with a record of good and bad deeds of all children, appeared as a Christmas picture in *Harper's*

Weekly. This was the first time that Christmas stockings were seen hanging from the fireplace mantel.

Santa Claus has different names in many other countries. In England he is known as Father Christmas. He looks much like the North American version of Santa Claus but he has a longer coat and a longer beard. In France his name is Père Noel, while in some South American countries he is Papa Noel. He is also known as Kris Kringle, Sinter Klaus or Grandfather Frost. Whatever his name, he is a magical figure and his arrival is awaited around the world each Christmas Eve.

In 1897, a young girl wrote a letter to the editor of the *New York Sun* asking if Santa Claus was real. The reply, written by Francis P. Church, remains a classic Christmas reading to this day.

Editorial page, New York Sun, 1897

We take great pleasure in answering thus prominently the communication below, expressing at the same time our great gratification that the faithful author is numbered among the friends of the *Sun*:

Dear Editor,

I am 8 years old. Some of my little friends say there is no Santa Claus. Papa says, "If you see it in *The Sun*, it's so." Please tell me the truth, is there a Santa Claus?

Virginia O'Hanlon

Virginia, your little friends are wrong. They have been affected by the skepticism of a skeptical age. They do not believe except that which they see. They think that nothing can be which is not comprehensible by their little minds. All minds, Virginia, whether they be men's or children's, are little. In this great universe of ours, man is a mere insect as compared with the boundless world about him, as measured by the intelligence capable of grasping the whole of truth and knowledge.

Yes, Virginia, there is a Santa Claus. He exists as certainly as love and generosity and devotion exist, and you know that they abound and give to your life its highest beauty and joy. Alas! How dreary would be the world if there were no Santa Claus! It would be as dreary as if there were no Virginias. There would be no childlike faith then, no poetry, no romance to make tolerable this existence. We should have no enjoyment, except in sense and sight. The external light with which childhood fills the world would be extinguished.

Not believe in Santa Claus! You might as well not believe in fairies. You might get your Papa to hire men to watch all the chimneys on Christmas Eve to catch Santa Claus, but even if you did not see Santa Claus coming down, what would that prove? Nobody sees Santa Claus, but that is no sign that there is no Santa Claus. The most real things in the world are those that neither children nor men can see. Did you ever see fairies dancing on the lawn? Of course not, but that is no proof that they are not there. Nobody can conceive or imagine all the wonders there are unseen and unseeable in the world.

You tear apart the baby's rattle and see what makes the noise inside, but there is a veil covering the unseen world which not the strongest man, nor even the united strength of all the strongest men that ever lived could tear apart. Only faith, poetry, love, romance can push aside that curtain and view and picture the supernatural beauty and glory beyond. Is it all real? Ah, Virginia, in all the world there is nothing else real and abiding.

No Santa Claus! Thank God! He lives and lives forever. A thousand years from now, Virginia, nay 10 times 10,000 years from now, he will continue to make glad the heart of childhood.

If you have young ones in the family, you will need to prepare a special snack to leave for Santa. (Don't forget to leave some vegetables for the reindeer, too.)

Orange Cranberry Delight Muffins

Santa seems to enjoy muffins when he visits our home. Here's a muffin recipe with a Christmas flavour.

2¼ cups (550 mL) all-purpose flour
2 tsp. (10 mL) baking powder
1 tsp. (5 mL) baking soda
½ tsp. (2 mL) salt

1 cup (250 mL) sugar
1 egg
½ cup (125 mL) milk
½ cup (125 mL) sour cream
⅓ cup (75 mL) canola oil
1½ cups (375 mL) fresh or frozen cranberries, chopped
1 tbsp. (15 mL) orange peel, grated
¼ cup (50 mL) whole cranberries

GLAZE

½ cup (125 mL) powdered sugar
1 tbsp. (15 mL) fresh orange juice
1 tsp. (5 mL) orange peel, grated

1. Preheat oven to 375°F (190°C). Line a 12-cup muffin tin with paper liners. Combine flour, baking powder, baking soda and salt in a medium bowl; make a well in the centre.
2. In a second bowl, mix together the sugar and the egg. Add milk, sour cream and oil and blend well. Pour batter into dry ingredients and mix until just moistened; do not over-mix. Fold in chopped cranberries and orange peel.
3. Fill liners about ¾ full. Place several whole cranberries on the top of each muffin. Bake 15 to 18

minutes or until muffins test done. While muffins are baking, stir together the glaze ingredients until smooth. Remove muffins from the pan and place on a wire rack. Brush glaze on warm muffins with a pastry brush. Cool and serve.

Makes 1 dozen muffins.

Bacon, Cheddar and Caraway Muffins

These muffins are delicious not only on Christmas Eve, but in the morning too, when they make a delightful morning snack for those who want to open gifts before breakfast.

2 cups (500 mL) flour, sifted
4 tsp. (20 mL) baking powder
4 oz. (125 g) sharp cheddar cheese, grated
8 slices crispy bacon, crumbled
2 tbsp. (30 mL) caraway seeds
¼ cup (50 mL) cooking oil
1 egg
pinch of salt
1½ to 2 cups (375 to 500 mL) milk

1. Preheat the oven to 400°F (200°C) and grease (or use paper liners) a 12-cup muffin pan.
2. Mix the sifted flour and baking powder in a large bowl. Add grated cheese, crumbled bacon and caraway seeds, then the oil, egg, salt and enough of the milk to form a dough with the consistency of runny porridge. Do not over-mix; the dough should be soft enough to pour. Spoon the mixture into the muffin pans. Sprinkle the top of each muffin with shreds of cheese for a glossy finish.
3. Bake for 10 to 12 minutes, until well risen and golden brown.

Makes 1 dozen large muffins.

The Miracle of Christmas

The miracle of Christmas
Is a wreath upon the door,
A Christmas tree in splendour
With gifts spread upon the floor,
A warm and glowing fire
In a cozy fireplace
And happy cheerful people
With a smile on every face.

The miracle of Christmas
Is a star-filled winter night
With window after window
Aglow with candlelight,
With patterns of purple shadows
Along the gleaming snow,
With happy youthful voices
Singing carols as they go.

The miracle of Christmas
Is a babe of long ago
And a gentle mother kneeling
By a manger crude and low,
And one star of glory shining
In the heavens up above
For the One who is the symbol
Of God's everlasting love.

V. G. Burns

The Christmas season often provides us with humorous events that make us laugh—even years later—when we tell and retell them to our children and grandchildren. Our daughter Julia is still embarrassed when we tell of her award-winning performance as Mary in the annual Christmas Eve pageant in the church. When the innkeeper announced, "We have no room in the inn," Julia gave him an almighty smack on the arm and in a loud, firm voice said, "I told you we need a room!"

The innkeeper, a rather whiny child, ran down the aisle to where his mother and father watched from the pew and sat down. Julia grabbed "Joseph" by the arm and dragged him over to the "stable," announcing to one and all, "Well, I guess this will just have to do, but I'm not happy about it!"

My grandson Marshall still breaks up laughing when we remind him of the Christmas Eve that he had to stay up all night to put together his daughter's bicycle. He hadn't noticed until too late that the only instructions were printed in Japanese!

Good friends of mine, Jim and Betty Lucas, have two wonderful stories that I'll share with you now. I'm sure you'll agree that these gems will remain in their family's "funniest ever" Christmas stories forever.

Tales of a Christmas Turkey

Betty and Jim and their four young children had recently moved to South America from New Jersey. Jim, an executive with the Ford Motor Company, had accepted a new position in Valencia, Venezuela, a small town about 30 miles south of Caracas. The town, nearly at the equator, was about as far as you could get from the cold, snowy, wintry Christmases that the family had known and loved.

Although the family had adapted pretty well to the dramatic change, the one thing they insisted upon was that they wanted a pavo (a turkey) for Christmas dinner. Not for them the tacos or pazoli (the soup that was popular Christmas fare in Venezuela). Jim had promised that the family would have a turkey dinner. (I believe he'd had to put it in writing before the family would agree to the move south.)

As Christmas came closer, Betty had managed to find a small Christmas tree, which she describes as a "pitiful little evergreen whose branches drooped miserably when the ornaments were hung."

Jim was having less success on the turkey front, however. There were about 54 English-speaking people in Valencia, and Jim's Spanish was in its beginning stage (i.e., he was incomprehensible to the natives). Realizing that success in finding a turkey in their small town was unlikely, he began to canvass the larger cities, like Caracas. It seemed that no one ate turkey. Finally Jim called back to the Ford company in Detroit and asked how he could get a turkey for Christmas.

Thus it was that a friend bought the largest turkey he

could find—a 28-pounder—which he packed in dry ice. The friend then took the turkey to the airport where it was placed, with great fanfare, in a first-class seat on a jet bound for Caracas, Venezuela.

Jim picked up the turkey on Christmas Eve and there was probably never a more well travelled, or more welcomed, bird at any Christmas dinner.

Some years later, Jim, who was still with the Ford Motor Company, was transferred to Mexico City. The family, by now accustomed to a warm-weather Christmas, still craved that one thing that was irreplaceable—the turkey.

Again, turkeys were not part of a Mexican Christmas dinner, but Betty knew that she could get a turkey at the market in Toluca, a village outside Mexico City. The "Witches Market" (so called because of the women there who sold many herbs and "magic" potions) was about an hour's bus ride from home. Betty convinced her 17-year-old son, Michael, to accompany her to the market. The two found the poultry seller and he was happy to show them the birds he had. The birds were all alive but Betty and Michael chose a plump one and asked the seller to dress the turkey. Although Betty and Michael's Spanish was relatively fluent, it took Betty a few minutes and much mime and gesturing to indicate that she wanted the bird plucked. At last the light dawned and the happy Mexican, eyes sparkling, nodded and said, "Si si Senora." He told Betty to come back in an hour. That gave Betty and Michael just enough time to collect the fruits, vegetables and pastries needed to complete the Christmas feast.

When Betty and Michael arrived back at the poultry seller's stall, he disappeared into the tent, reappearing almost immediately with the turkey. This poor bird came straggling out of the tent, as alive as it had ever been—but completely plucked of all its feathers. It gave a rather pitiful "Gobble, gobble . . ." as Betty and Michael looked on in stupefaction.

By now quite a crowd had gathered around the naked bird and the astonished Mexicans were laughing till tears ran down their faces.

When Betty made it understood that she wanted the bird killed, the seller shrugged his shoulders and gave her a look that said "Why didn't you say this an hour ago?"

Eventually Michael and Betty arrived home with the now dead and plucked bird but they had a difficult time eating a turkey with whom they felt so intimately connected.

The Heart Goes Home

Always the heart goes home on Christmas Eve . . .
Goes silently across the continent,
Or mountains or the sea. A heart will leave
The glitter of a city street, and sent
By something deep and timeless, find the way
To a little cottage on a country hill.
And even if the little cottage may
Have disappeared, a heart will find it still . . .

The smile of tenderness upon the faces,
The simple words, the arms secure and strong,
The sweetness of the well-remembered places . . .

All these a heart will find and will belong
Once more to country hills, however far,
And sense the holy presence of the Star.

Grace V. Watkins

Christmas Eve

Christmas Eve is a night of delightful celebrations. It is a time for visitors: friends, relatives and neighbours come to share the warm spirit of this special night. Children hang their stockings and then rush to bed, where they listen intently for the tinkle of sleigh bells or the sounds of reindeer hooves upon the roof that signal Santa's arrival.

Most families have special rituals that they enjoy on the night before Christmas. For our family, it's a time for last-minute gift wrapping, for catching up on all the news since our last gathering, and for attending the candlelight service at our church.

My husband, George, always made a traditional, east-coast chowder for our supper on Christmas Eve.

This recipe, which came from his mother, has been passed down and now my grandson Marshall has mastered this culinary delight.

'Twas the night before Christmas

And all through the house . . .

Salt Cod Chowder

This soup brings the east coast back to us wherever we may be!

1 lb. (500 g) salt codfish
6 slices of salt pork, ¼ inch (5 mm) thick, diced
8 medium potatoes, peeled and diced
4 medium onions, peeled and diced
10 cups (2.5 L) milk
2 cups (500 mL) cream
salt and pepper to taste

1. Flake the codfish and soak in lukewarm water until the fish is soft and the salt has been removed. Drain and discard the water.
2. Fry the pork in a large heavy saucepan. When the pork is golden brown, add potatoes, onions and codfish. Simmer gently in as little water as possible for about 20 minutes or until the fish and vegetables are tender. Add the milk, cream and salt and pepper to taste, and heat until hot but not boiling. Transfer to a large, warmed soup tureen.

Makes 10 to 12 servings.

Many of our friends like to have a fondue on Christmas Eve. The nicest thing about fondue is that preparation is minimal and this type of dinner allows everyone a chance to relax and enjoy each other's company. Children, in particular, seem to love a fondue meal and my great-grandchildren have even been known to eat any number of vegetables when dipped in a cheese fondue (Justin used to consider ketchup and relish as two vegetable servings).

Back in the 1960s, fondue dinners were a cheap but cosmopolitan way to entertain. This type of meal made a comeback in the late 90s and right through to the present time.

Fondue was invented centuries ago by Swiss villagers living in isolated regions. During the long winter months, supplies were scarce and every scrap had to be used. Fondue was a way to use up dried cheese and stale bread.

The classic Swiss cheese fondue is a combination of Gruyère and Emmenthaler cheeses but many regions have their own variations. The oil fondue, in which you dip meats, is said to have originated in the vineyards of Burgundy. Legend has it that vineyard owners heated vats of grapeseed oil in the fields so that the workers could eat on the job (dipping meats brought from home) and then get quickly back to work.

If you are new to fondue cooking, here are a few tips to make your meal a success.

1. Use pots and fuel according to the manufacturer's directions.
2. Use the right kind of pot for cheese-, oil- or broth-based fondues and chocolate fondues. Usually ceramic pots are used for cheese and chocolate while metal pots are ideal for oil and broth fondues.
3. When serving a chocolate fondue, the chocolate will coat fruits better if the fruit is chilled. The chocolate is better served warm than hot to avoid burning the chocolate (or your mouth).
4. Use a dry wine in a cheese fondue. If the cheese separates, keep stirring. If the cheese curdles, add a teaspoon of lemon juice and stir well.
5. Do not use fresh bread for dipping; it will fall apart in the fondue.

Traditional Swiss Cheese Fondue

1½ cups (375 mL) dry white wine
1 tbsp. (15 mL) lemon juice
1 clove garlic
3 cups (750 mL) Gruyère cheese, shredded
3 cups (750 mL) Emmenthaler cheese, shredded

1 tbsp. (15 mL) cornstarch
2 tbsp. (30 mL) kirsch
pinch of salt
¼ tsp. (1 mL) paprika
¼ tsp. (1 mL) grated nutmeg

1. In a saucepan, bring the wine, lemon juice and garlic to a boil over medium heat. Reduce heat to medium-low; remove garlic.
2. In a bowl, toss together Gruyère and Emmenthaler cheeses and cornstarch; gradually add this mixture to the liquid in the saucepan, a handful at a time, whisking constantly until the cheese melts before adding more cheese. Cook until mixture is thickened and starting to bubble; add kirsch, salt, paprika and nutmeg. Stir and transfer the mixture to the fondue pot set over a fondue burner.
3. For dipping, prepare a selection of vegetables—broccoli, cauliflower, mushrooms and sweet peppers; add cubed bread to dip and you'll have a wonderful Christmas Eve meal.

O Holy Night!

O Holy Night! The stars are brightly shining
It is the night of our dear Saviour's birth!

Chocolate Fondue

For a super dessert, a chocolate fondue is just the thing.

8 oz. (250 g) semi-sweet baking chocolate
1 cup (250 mL) whipping cream
3 to 4 tbsp. (45 to 60 mL) rum or Cointreau
1 tbsp. (15 mL) granulated brown sugar (optional)

1. Break the chocolate into small pieces, put it in the fondue pot and pour in the cream, rum (or Cointreau) and sugar (if using it).
2. Cook on the stove over medium-low heat, stirring frequently until the chocolate is melted and the ingredients are thoroughly blended. Transfer the fondue pot to the lighted burner and serve a variety of chilled fruits such as whole strawberries, banana slices, orange segments or pineapple cubes. Small pieces of biscotti or stale angel food cake are also good dippers.

The Christmas Eve service is truly one of my favourites of the year. In our church we have the children's presentation of the Christmas story and then, as the children return to sit with their families, we sing some of the best-loved carols.

For French-Canadian families, Christmas Eve is a time for joyous revelry. The midnight Mass, or "Minuette," is celebrated, after which the family returns home for the *reveillon*, a time of feasting, gifts, dancing, storytelling and games. It is often the tradition, after gifts have been opened, to enjoy a tortière, a pork pie that is a specialty in Quebec.

Tortière

Good friends of ours, Paul and Madeleine Pouliot, lived in Quebec City and Madeleine's recipe for tortière is certainly my favourite.

1 lb. (500 g) lean ground pork or
½ lb. (250 g) each lean ground beef and ground pork
1 onion, chopped fine
1 tsp. (5 mL) minced garlic
2 tbsp. (30 mL) parsley flakes
½ tsp. (2 mL) salt

½ tsp. (2 mL) savory
¼ tsp. (1 mL) celery salt
¼ tsp. (1 mL) ground cloves
½ cup (125 mL) water or beef broth
½ cup (125 mL) bread crumbs

Pastry for 9-inch (22.5-cm) double crust pie
1 egg beaten with 1 tsp. (5 mL) water

1. In a large skillet or saucepan, mix together the beef and pork. Add remaining ingredients (except bread crumbs, pastry and egg) and bring to a boil. Lower heat and simmer mixture for 20 minutes.
2. Add the bread crumbs spoonful by spoonful, stirring until fat has been absorbed. Cool the mixture.
3. Preheat oven to 375°F (190°C). Spoon mixture into the uncooked pie shell. Moisten the rim of the pie shell with water. Cover the pie with the top pastry, pressing the edges together to seal. Trim and flute the pastry edge.
4. Combine the egg with 1 tsp. (5 mL) water; brush it over the crust. You can make small decorative shapes with the trimmed pastry and arrange them on top. Brush the decorations with some of the remaining egg mixture. Cut steam vent holes in top.

5. Bake for 40 to 45 minutes or until golden brown. Cool for 10 minutes before serving.

Serves 8.

The last thing we do before going to bed on Christmas Eve is hang our stockings on the fireplace.

The stockings were hung by the chimney with care,
In hopes that Saint Nicholas soon would be there.

Here in North America, the traditional Christmas stocking harkens back to those lines from the poem by Clement C. Moore, "A Visit from Saint Nicholas." As mentioned earlier, it was the illustration by Thomas Nast that first showed stockings being hung from the mantel.

In Holland, during the 16th century, children would leave their wooden clogs by the hearth. They filled them with straw for the reindeer, and a treat for Santa

(Sinter-Klaus) was left in the house near the warm fire. In turn, Sinter-Klaus would leave treats for the children.

Children who live in countries that celebrate Christmas continue the tradition of leaving stockings or shoes out for Santa to fill. In France, children place their shoes by the fireplace, as do the children who live today in Holland. In Hungary, children shine their shoes before placing them near the door or on a window sill.

Italian children leave their shoes out the night before Epiphany, January 5, for La Befana, the good witch. In Puerto Rico children put greenery and flowers in small boxes and place them under their beds for the camels of the Three Kings.

As youngsters, we were told that if we were not good children, our stockings would be filled with coal instead of with treats. Happily, we never had a coal-filled stocking.

The Christmas stocking!
How endearing to childhood's joy
To find it bulging on Christmas morning
With candy and nuts and a toy.

A. Schneider

Christmas Eve is also the time that we usually set the dining-room table for Christmas dinner. If ever there is a time to use your best china, crystal and silver, this would most certainly be it. Even if you have none of these things, you can make the table special in many ways. Inexpensive cotton Christmas material can be used to make placemats and napkins that look quite lovely on a plain white tablecloth. Fresh flowers combined with pine cones, pine boughs, holly or mistletoe branches make any table look festive.

Add as many candles as will fit and you'll have a beautiful table that will make the dinner a memorable one.

Another lovely centrepiece can be made by decorating a large crystal or clear glass bowl. Line the bowl with greenery and then fill it with coloured glass ornaments. Surround the bowl with red or white candles in votive holders for a beautiful effect.

Our table is always set with Christmas crackers, a tradition that comes from our British heritage. Tom Smith, a Victorian confectioner's apprentice, invented this popular favour—a paper cylinder containing a message of endearment, small candies and a saltpetre friction strip to add a bang when it's pulled open.

Today's crackers contain a rhyme, riddle or joke, a paper hat and a small gift, and they still bang when they are opened. The more expensive the cracker, the better the gift.

My friend Martha has a unique way of decorating

her Christmas table. She has a number of home-made quilts, one of them being red and white. She uses her quilt as a tablecloth, adding red placemats and napkins. Her centrepiece is a tiny evergreen planted in a painted pot. Tiny decorations and glitter sprinkled on the tree make this a very special and cherished tradition.

When Christmas is over, the quilt goes back on the bed and the tree is planted on the family property.

And there were in the same country shepherds abiding in the field, keeping watch over the flock by night. And Lo! The angel of the Lord came upon them and the glory of the Lord shone round about them: and they were sore afraid. And the angel said unto them, "Fear not: for behold, I bring good tidings of great joy, which shall be to all people.

"For unto you is born this day in the city of David, a saviour, which is Christ the Lord." And suddenly there was with the angel a multitude of the heavenly host praising God and saying "Glory be to God in the highest, and on earth peace, goodwill towards men."

Luke 2:8–11, 13, 14

The people that walked in the darkness have seen a light; they that dwell in the land of the shadow of death, upon them hath the light shined.

For unto us a child is born, unto us a son is given: and the government shall be upon his shoulder: and his name shall be called

Wonderful
Counselor
The Mighty God
The Everlasting Father
The Prince of Peace

Isaiah 9:1, 6

Hark! The Herald Angels sing "Glory to the new-born King!"

Christmas Morning

Christians awake!
Salute the happy morn,
Whereon the Saviour
Of the world was born!

Christmas morning! What a joyous and happy time it is for all of us—young and old alike. Every family seems to have its own rituals for this special day but in our family we follow a routine that originated when my sister, Sarah, my brother Ben and I were youngsters.

As a child I usually woke up early and had to wait for my father to begin our trip to the living room; when I had my own children, we maintained this tradition, waiting to hear George's voice echoing up to the girls and me, "My heavens! Look what Santa has brought this year!"

In the next generation, a similar routing is still followed. Although the children would like to tiptoe downstairs to see what Santa has delivered, no one is allowed to go down before my son-in-law Bruce turns on the tree lights—and that doesn't happen before 7:00 a.m.

Stocking gifts are opened first, and then we exchange our gifts with one another. When we have all oohed and aahed over our presents, it's time to have breakfast before we ready ourselves for church. Breakfast for us is a substantial meal as we don't eat again until dinner at around four in the afternoon.

We have a number of delicious (and filling) breakfast dishes, some of which can be made ahead of time, allowing everyone—even the cook—to relax before starting on the dinner feast.

Special French Toast

This recipe comes from my son-in-law John. He has made French toast for years with his special syrup, and everyone comes back for seconds!

12 ¾-inch (2-cm) thick slices of French bread
3 tbsp. (45 mL) unsalted butter

BATTER
6 large eggs
1½ cups (375 mL) whipping cream

1½ tbsp. (22 mL) vanilla extract
2 tsp. (10 mL) cinnamon
¾ tsp. (3 mL) grated nutmeg

SYRUP

2 cups (500 mL) maple syrup
1 cup (250 mL) honey
1 tbsp. (15 mL) vanilla
1 cup (250 mL) sliced almonds, lightly toasted
1 cup (250 mL) dried mixed fruits, such as apples, apricots, raisins and peaches
fresh fruit for garnish

1. Make the syrup first. In a saucepan warm the maple syrup, honey and vanilla over medium-low heat, stirring often. Add nuts and dried fruit. Bring mixture to a boil and remove the pan from the heat.
2. To make the batter, whisk all ingredients together in a large bowl until they are well blended.
3. In a large non-stick pan, heat 1 tbsp. (15 mL) of the butter over moderate heat until melted. Dip bread slices into the batter and let excess drip off. Cook in batches until crisp and golden, about 2 minutes per side, adding remaining butter to the pan as needed. Transfer the toast, as it is cooked, to paper

towels to drain. Serve French toast warm with the syrup and fresh fruit for garnish.

Makes 6 servings.

My great-grandson Michael, who likes his food "just plain, Grammie," prefers to have his French toast served with plain maple syrup and fresh peaches. He insists that it is every bit as delicious his way.

Ham and Cheese Strata

Another popular dish in our family is this make-ahead recipe.

2 tbsp. (30 mL) Dijon mustard
12 slices of bread, crusts removed
6 slices deli ham
1½ cups (375 mL) sharp Cheddar cheese, shredded
9 large eggs
3 cups (750 mL) whole milk
½ tsp. (2 mL) salt
¼ tsp. (1 mL) freshly ground black pepper

1. Grease a 13" × 9" (22 × 33 cm) ceramic or glass baking dish.
2. Spread mustard on one side of each bread slice. Arrange 6 slices mustard side up in the bottom of the baking dish. Cover each slice with a slice of ham and then with the shredded cheese. Cover with the remaining 6 bread slices, mustard side down.
3. In a bowl and using a wire whisk, beat together the eggs, milk, salt and pepper until well blended. Slowly pour the egg mixture over the bread slices. Let stand overnight, then bake at 350°F (180°C) for 45 minutes to 1 hour or until puffed and golden and a knife inserted into the centre comes out clean. Let stand 10 minutes before serving.

Makes 6 servings.

Curried Fruit

My dear friend Elaine who lives in Shelburne, Ontario, serves the strata each Christmas morning with curried fruit. Everyone loves this delicious dish that complements the strata so well!

1 small can peaches
1 small can pears
1 small can pineapple rings
¼ cup (50 mL) maraschino cherries
½ cup (375 mL) melted butter
½ cup (125 mL) brown sugar
2 tbsp. (30 mL) cornstarch
2 tsp. (10 mL) curry powder

1. Heat oven to 350°F (180°C). In an oven-proof glass casserole dish, mix the fruit together.
2. In another bowl, mix the remaining ingredients together. Pour this sauce over the fruit and bake for 1 hour. (You can bake the sandwiches and the fruit together as the time works well.)

Dear friends of ours are Jewish and they celebrate Hanukkah around the time of the winter solstice. A traditional Hanukkah treat, homemade jelly doughnuts, has found its way into our family list of Christmas morning favourites.

Jelly Doughnuts

If this seems like too much work for Christmas morning, there's always Boxing Day.

¾ cup (175 mL) warm milk
1 pkg. (¼ oz./7 g) active dry yeast
3 cups (750 mL) all-purpose flour, setting ¾ cup (175 mL) aside separately
1 tsp. (5 mL) grated lemon zest
¾ tsp. (3 mL) ground cinnamon
¾ tsp. (3 mL) salt
¼ tsp. (1 mL) ground nutmeg
⅓ cup (75 mL) butter (or margarine) at room temperature
⅓ cup (75 mL) granulated sugar
3 eggs
1½ tsp. (7 mL) vanilla extract
½ cup (125 mL) jelly or seedless jam (raspberry, strawberry or grape work well)
confectioner's sugar

1. In a bowl, combine milk and yeast; let stand until foamy (for about 5 minutes). Stir in ¾ cup (175 mL) flour until a sticky batter forms. Cover the bowl with plastic wrap; let stand in a warm place until risen and spongy, for about 30 minutes.

2. Meanwhile combine the remaining flour with zest, cinnamon, salt and nutmeg, and set the mixture aside.
3. In a large bowl with mixer on high speed, beat butter and granulated sugar until light and fluffy. Beat in eggs and vanilla. Using a spoon, stir in the yeast mixture until combined. Stir in the flour mixture until a soft, sticky dough forms. Coat a large bowl with non-stick cooking spray and transfer dough to a bowl. Cover the bowl with plastic wrap and let it stand in a warm place until the dough doubles in size (about 1 hour). I know this seems like a lot of work, but keep going—it's worth it!
4. While dough is rising, set out a cookie sheet and line it with several layers of paper towel. Place a wire rack over the paper towels to prepare a place for the doughnuts to cool.
5. In an electric fry pan (or heavy skillet), heat about 1 inch (2.5 cm) of canola oil to 350°F (180°C). (You can also use a deep fryer with oil heated to 350°F/180°C.)
6. With lightly floured hands, punch down the dough. Turn dough out onto floured surface (dough will be sticky) and lightly sprinkle the top of the dough with flour. Roll out the dough to a ½-inch (1-cm) thickness, sprinkling the dough with flour as needed to prevent sticking. With a 3-

inch (8-cm) round cutter, cut out 12 circles, re-rolling the scraps.

7. In small batches, gently drop the doughnuts into the oil. Fry, turning once, until doughnuts are puffed and golden (2 to 4 minutes per side). Remove with slotted spoon. Drain on racks; cool. If using a deep fat fryer, follow the manufacturer's directions for frying doughnuts.
8. When doughnuts are cool, push the handle of a wooden spoon into the side of the doughnut to make a hole. Do not push the handle right through.

   Spoon jelly into a plastic sandwich bag and snip one corner. Squeeze about 2 tbsp. (30 mL) of jelly into the hole in each doughnut. Sprinkle confectioner's sugar on each doughnut and serve.

Makes about one dozen doughnuts.

After breakfast on Christmas morning, I like to spend a little time alone. It's then that I can think back to happy Christmas Days past and I remember my wonderful husband, George, and the good times that we shared. I know how proud he would be of our children, grandchildren and great-grandchildren, seeing what wonderful people they have become.

When you have lost a loved one, Christmas can be a difficult time. The following lines bring me comfort:

Tenderly we treasure the past,
With loving memories that will always last.

Christmas Dinner

Good Christian men rejoice
With heart and soul and voice;
Give ye heed to what we say;
News! News!

Jesus Christ is born today;
Ox and ass before him bow,
And He is in the manger now.
Christ is born today!
Christ is born today!

Each of us has special memories from childhood Christmases and, although my childhood may be much further away than yours, the happy times come back to me so quickly.

I have probably told this story many times but perhaps you'll remember a special Christmas of your own as you read it.

When I was young, I used to look forward, all year, to Christmas dinner at Grandma and Grandpa's house. I loved to see all my cousins and aunts and uncles, but I had two particular favourites. Uncle Bill and Uncle Harry, my mother's two brothers-in-law, were such fun. They each had a tremendous sense of humour and I found everything they said absolutely hilarious.

Uncle Bill would say something really funny, and Uncle Harry and I would laugh uproariously. Uncle Harry had the most wonderful laugh I have ever heard! It would come up from somewhere near his toes, I think, and just exploded out of him. I have seen entire rooms full of people break up with laughter and have no idea what they were laughing at. That is how terrific Uncle Harry's laugh was.

One Christmas in particular, my dad and my two uncles decided to see who could eat the most. They didn't tell anyone else, but I had overheard them talking in the living room.

"I believe I'll have more turkey, Mother MacIntosh," said Uncle Bill. "Yes, I will too," said Dad and Uncle Harry.

It went on and on. Most of the other children had been excused from the dining room but I was anxious to see who would win, so I hung about quietly, so as not to be noticed.

"My word, I think I'm going to explode!" Uncle Harry moaned.

There's No Place Like Home for the Holidays

Oh, there's no place like home for the holidays
'Cause no matter how far away you roam
When you pine for the sunshine of a friendly gaze
For the holidays you can't beat home sweet home

Well, that was too much for me to see alone, so I raced off to get the others. "Come quickly, Uncle Harry's going to explode!" I yelled.

We all raced back to the dining room to wait for the impending combustion. When Uncle Harry found out why we were all staring at him, his laugh came bellowing out of him and we were all part of the huge joke.

These were wonderful times for me and made for cherished memories that have stayed with me for my lifetime.

Most of us work very hard to make our Christmas dinner memorable. Sometimes it can be more unforgettable than we'd like it to be. This story was told to me by my dear friends Pat and Ian Brown of Ottawa.

Pat and Ian's son Geoff and his wife, Louise, worked and lived in Europe for a number of years. One Christmas, Geoff and Louise were living in Belgium. As a present, the couple sent airline tickets to Pat and Ian so that the four of them could enjoy a family Christmas in Belgium.

Pat and Ian arrived several days before Christmas, and the four of them had a wonderful time getting ready for this very special Christmas day to be spent together.

Louise, knowing how much her British-born in-laws enjoyed a traditional dinner, had visited her local butcher to order a large turkey. Turkey is not usually a part of the Belgian meal but the butcher assured her that she would indeed have her turkey on Christmas Eve.

On December 24, Louise arrived at the meat shop at the appointed hour and was greeted by the smiling butcher. Louise asked for the turkey and the man came forward carrying a package wrapped in brown paper. Louise eyed the package quizzically and asked, "What is this?" The package was about 18 inches long but only 4 inches thick, very un-turkey–like in shape.

The butcher proudly unwrapped the paper to reveal a turkey—minus every single one of its bones.

Louise was nearly in tears. "Oh my gosh," she said about ten times. "My mother-in-law is here and she's expecting a turkey dinner."

The poor bewildered butcher, who had worked so hard for hours de-boning the bird, had no idea what was wrong.

After determining that there was not another turkey to be had, Louise was left with no other alternative than to wrap up the turkey meat and take it home.

When Louise arrived home and unwrapped the "turkey," all four of them collapsed on the couch laughing until they had tears running down their cheeks. Louise, however, was not ready to give up. On

Christmas morning she set about making stuffing—mountains of it. She then packed the stuffing into the roasting pan doing her best to fashion it into a turkey shape. The turkey meat was then placed on the dressing—even wrapped around wooden sticks to make legs and wings. When she had finished, the pile of meat and dressing actually bore a striking resemblance to a real turkey.

This is one dinner that will be long remembered!

For many years a goose was the most popular bird to serve at the Christmas dinner table.

I'm sure you will remember the scene in Charles Dickens' "A Christmas Carol" where he describes Christmas dinner at the home of the Cratchits (including Tiny Tim):

> *Such a bustle ensued that you might have thought a goose the rarest of all birds; a feathered phenomenon, to which a black swan was a matter of course—and in truth it was something very like it in that house . . . At last the dishes were set on, and grace was said . . . There never was such a goose. Bob said he didn't believe there ever was such a goose cooked. Its tenderness and flavour, size and cheapness, were the themes of universal admiration.*

Since many North American traditions arrived here from Britain, the goose preceded the turkey as the bird of the Christmas feast.

Some families still enjoy a roast goose, and this recipe for wild rice and chestnut stuffing is just about the best goose stuffing I've ever tasted.

Wild Rice and Chestnut Stuffing

2 tbsp. (30 mL) butter or margarine
1 Granny Smith apple, peeled, cored and chopped
1 large stalk of celery, diced
1 medium carrot, diced
1 small onion, diced
½ tsp. (2 mL) salt
¼ tsp. (1 mL) pepper
¼ tsp. (1 mL) thyme leaves
2 10-oz. (398-mL) cans chicken broth
1 4-oz. (100-g) pkg. wild rice
1 cup (250 mL) parboiled rice
1 lb. (500 g) chestnuts

1. In a 3-quart (3-L) saucepan, melt 1 tbsp. (15 mL) butter or margarine. Add the apple pieces and cook until softened. With a slotted spoon, remove

the cooked apple to a small bowl and set aside. Melt 1 tbsp. (15 mL) butter in the same saucepan; add celery, carrot, onion, salt, pepper and thyme. Cook until vegetables are tender crisp and golden.

2. Over high heat, stir in chicken broth, water, wild rice and the parboiled rice and bring to a boil. Reduce heat to low and simmer for 25 minutes or until the liquid is absorbed and white and wild rice are tender.
3. While rice is cooking, prepare chestnuts. Put chestnuts in a 4-quart (4-L) saucepan with enough water to cover. Bring water to a boil, and reduce heat to medium; cook for 10 minutes. Remove the chestnuts 2 or 3 at a time to a cutting board; cut each in half and scrape out the meat. When rice is cooked, stir in the cooked apple and chestnut meat. Set aside as you prepare the goose.

Roast Goose with Chestnut Stuffing

1 goose, 10 to 12 lbs. (4.5 to 5.5 kg)
½ lemon
salt and pepper
½ cup (125 mL) red wine, warmed

1. Preheat oven to 400°F (200°C). Remove the neck and giblets from the bird's cavity. Pull off any loose fat from the cavity and around the neck. Wash the bird inside and out. Drain well and dry thoroughly with a cloth. Rub the goose inside and out with the lemon half and squeeze the juice over the bird as you work.
2. Sprinkle the body cavity lightly with salt and pepper.
3. Stuff the neck cavity with a portion of the chestnut-rice stuffing. Fasten the neck skin to the body with a skewer.
4. Stuff the body cavity with the remaining stuffing and skewer or sew shut. Tie legs and wings close to the body. With a skewer gently prick the skin all over the bird to allow fat to escape during roasting.
5. Place the goose breast side down on a greased rack in a shallow roasting pan. Pour 2 cups (500 mL) boiling water over the bird. Roast uncovered at 400°F

(200 °C) for 20 minutes. Reduce heat to 325 °F (160 °C) and continue roasting for one hour.

6. Pour off and discard pan drippings. Baste the goose with ¼ cup (50 mL) warmed wine. Turn goose over; prick again with skewer. Pour another 2 cups (500 mL) boiling water over the bird. Roast, breast side up, for 1 hour.
7. Pour off and discard pan drippings. Baste goose with remaining wine and roast another 1 to 1½ hours. When done, the goose should be nicely browned, the drumsticks should move slightly in their sockets and, when the goose is pierced with a skewer, the juice should be a clear pale yellow.
8. Transfer the goose to the carving board. Cover loosely with foil and allow to stand for 15 minutes before carving. Remove skewers and string. Transfer stuffing to a serving bowl and keep warm while carving. Place carved meat on a serving platter and serve with rice and chestnut stuffing.

Makes about 12 servings.

For those of us who enjoy the traditional Christmas turkey, there are any number of stuffing recipes to choose from.

Cornbread-Sausage Stuffing

This recipe comes from my friend Emily and it has a definite taste of the south. If you enjoy spicy food, this stuffing is for you.

2 pkgs. (8½ oz./250 g each) cornbread mix
1 red pepper, cut into ½" (1 cm) pieces
1 or 2 jalapeños, seeded and minced
2 tsp. (10 mL) Cajun seasoning, such as Louisiana Style
½ tsp. (2 mL) dried sage
1 tbsp. (15 mL) parsley flakes
⅔ cup (150 mL) half and half cream
3 eggs
1 pkg. (12 oz./375 g) frozen bulk breakfast sausage, thawed
2 cups (500 mL) frozen corn, thawed
6 to 8 scallions, chopped (about 1½ cups/375 mL)

1. Preheat oven to 400°F (200°C). Coat a 13" × 9" (33 × 22 cm) baking pan with cooking spray. In a bowl, combine cornbread mix, red pepper, jalapeños, Cajun seasoning, sage and parsley flakes.
2. Whisk the cream with 2 eggs. Stir the cream mixture into the cornbread mixture until combined. Spread batter evenly into the pan. Bake for 25 minutes or until a toothpick comes out clean.

3. Cool completely in pan on a rack. Break cornbread into pieces; if too moist, put pieces on a baking sheet in the oven for 2 to 3 minutes or until dry.
4. Put sausage in a large skillet over medium high heat. Break it into small pieces and cook until no longer pink.
5. In a large bowl, combine cornbread pieces, sausage, corn and scallions. Whisk remaining egg with ½ cup (125 mL) water; stir into cornbread mixture until moistened. Cover and refrigerate until ready to stuff the turkey.

Enough for up to 15 lb. (6.5 kg) turkey.

Sarah's Stuffing

This recipe also combines sausage but it is a more traditional stuffing with a great combination of sausage, apples and sage. This is the stuffing my sister, Sarah, prefers, and using a package stuffing makes it a little more convenient.

12 oz. (375 g) bulk breakfast sausage
1 egg
1 pkg. (14 oz./440 g) cubed herb seasoned stuffing

3 apples unpeeled, coarsely chopped (Rome apples work well)
2 celery ribs (chopped, about 1 cup / 250 mL)
1 medium onion, chopped (about 1 cup / 250 mL)
½ cup (125 mL) butter or margarine, melted
1 tsp. (5 mL) pepper
1 can (10 oz. / 398 mL) chicken broth
¼ cup (50 mL) chopped fresh parsley
1 tsp. (5 mL) dried sage
½ tsp. (2 mL) dried thyme
½ tsp. (2 mL) dried savory

1. In a skillet over medium heat, cook sausage until browned and no longer pink (7 to 10 minutes). Drain off fat.
2. In a bowl, lightly beat the egg; stir in the package of stuffing, apples, celery, onion, butter, pepper and sausage. Slowly add broth, parsley, sage, thyme and savory. Stir together to mix well. Refrigerate until ready to stuff the turkey.

Enough for a 12 to 14 lb. (5.5 to 6.5 kg) turkey.

Cranberry-Orange Stuffing

This stuffing is one that my daughter Marg likes to use. It has been a hit with our family for many years.

6 cups (1.5 L) stale bread cubes
1 tsp. (5 mL) salt
½ tsp. (2 mL) pepper
½ tsp. (2 mL) each of dried thyme, sage and savory
2 tbsp. (30 mL) chopped parsley
1 cup (250 mL) chopped onion
⅓ cup (75 mL) butter
1 cup (250 mL) fresh or frozen (thawed) cranberries
2 oranges, peeled and chopped
1 can (10 oz./398 mL) chicken broth

1. Combine bread, salt, pepper, thyme, sage, savory and parsley in a large bowl. Mix together well.
2. Sauté the onions in the butter just until onions are transparent (about 7 minutes).
3. Combine the onions and butter with the bread mixture.
4. Add cranberries and orange pieces (including any juice from chopping the oranges) to the bread mixture.
5. Pour the chicken broth into the mixture and stir.

The stuffing mixture should hold together. If it seems too dry, add enough water that the mixture holds together lightly but not so much that it makes the mixture wet.
Refrigerate until ready to stuff the turkey.

Enough for a 12 to 14 lb. (5.5 to 6.5 kg) turkey

With any stuffing recipe, you can double the amounts for a larger bird. Any leftover stuffing can be baked in a covered casserole dish in the oven and served as an extra side dish with dinner. If the stuffing dries out, simply add more broth or water as it bakes.

Writing about making stuffing reminded me of a funny story that came from friends several years ago. Glenna and Richard Dimmig's son Jason was visiting with friends in the ski resort area of Lake Louise, Alberta. It was in late November, the time that Americans celebrate their Thanksgiving Day. Jason, a native of Pennsylvania, decided to surprise his friends with a Thanksgiving feast. While they were at work, he would put together a turkey dinner with all the trimmings. There was only one tiny flaw in this plan: Jason had no idea how to cook anything much past boiled eggs or macaroni. Undeterred, he phoned his mother and thus began one of the longest long-distance telephone cooking lessons in history. Glenna led Jason step by step as he made stuffing, roast turkey, mashed potatoes, gravy and the pièce de resistance, a pumpkin pie.

In fact, for the price of the telephone call, Jason could probably have taken the group to a high-class restaurant for dinner. However, the look on the faces of his friends as he presented his elegant feast (they had eaten a few of Jason's previous offerings) was priceless.

Roasting the Turkey

1. Wipe the turkey inside and out with a small cloth wrung out with warm water. Lightly salt the body cavity and the neck end and fill with your favourite stuffing. Do not pack tightly.
2. Place the turkey on a rack in the roaster. Season the skin lightly with salt and pepper and lay strips of bacon over the breast. (The bacon is optional but I like the extra flavour it adds.) Cover the roasting pan with a tent of foil—ensure a tight seal around the pan.
3. Cooking time is about 20 minutes per pound (half

kilogram) at 325°F (160°C). Remove the foil and the bacon strips for the final half hour to allow the turkey to brown. To test that the bird is cooked, pierce the thick part of the thigh with a fine skewer. The juices should run clear with no trace of pink.

The dinner bell is ringing
As each one takes his place,
And a glimpse of festive glory
Adorns each happy face.

With heart-felt thanks for the Holy Child
On this Christmas holiday,
We bow our heads in reverence,
In the good old fashioned way.

Author Unknown

My husband, George, as wonderful and accomplished a man as he was, never fully mastered the art of carving the turkey. George was good-natured about his shortcoming and was often the first to mention that our bird usually looked as if it had been blown up. I'll bet he would have appreciated these tips that my friend Jake Frampton passed along.

Carving the Turkey

1. Remove the leg and thigh quarter. Slice through the skin that holds the thigh to the turkey. To locate the joint, pull the leg away from the turkey. Cut the tendons between the bones that hold the joint together and remove the leg.
2. Cut through the joint that connects the thigh to the drumstick. You can serve the drumstick as is or slice the meat from the bone. Slice meat from the thigh.
3. Cut through the skin between wing and breast, locate the joint and then cut through as in step 1.
4. To cut slices of meat from the breast, hold the breast with a fork and slice downward against the grain of the meat. Carving the slices thinly makes the cutting easier.

Although we are a family of turkey lovers, there are a few misguided souls who actually do not care for turkey. For some of my friends, nothing beats a prime rib roast on their festive table.

Herb-Crusted Rib Roast

My friend Muriel sent along this delicious recipe for a herb-crusted rib roast. This is a sure winner for any special occasion.

7 to 8 lb. (3 to 3.5 kg) beef rib roast
cooking spray
2 tbsp. (30 mL) steak seasoning
1¾ tsp. (8 mL) dried rosemary, with ¼ tsp. (1 mL) set aside
¼ tsp. (1 mL) dried tarragon leaves
1 tsp. (5 mL) dried parsley flakes
1 medium head of garlic
¼ cup (50 mL) red wine
1 jar of beef gravy (12 oz./375 mL)

1. Pre-heat oven to 425°F (220°C). Place roast, fat side up, on a rack in a large roasting pan. Coat the top with cooking spray. Mix together the steak seasoning, 1½ tsp. (7 mL) rosemary, tarragon, and parsley flakes and sprinkle on the roast top. Press the herbs into the roast.
2. Remove any loose papery leaves from the garlic, and cut off the top ⅓ from the garlic head and discard it. Coat garlic with cooking spray and wrap it in foil. Place garlic and beef in the oven. Reduce oven temperature to 350°F (180°C). Roast garlic until cloves are very soft (35 to 45 minutes). Remove garlic from oven and cool. Roast beef until meat thermometer registers 140°F (60°C) (medium rare), about 2 hours. Let stand for 10 minutes before slicing.

3. Meanwhile, squeeze garlic pulp from cloves. Press pulp through a strainer and reserve.
4. For gravy, skim off the fat from the juices in the pan. Place the pan over low heat and stir in the red wine. Stir, scraping browned bits from the bottom of the pan and heat until hot (about 1 minute). Increase the heat to medium; pour in the jar of gravy; add reserved garlic and remaining rosemary. Bring to a boil, then reduce the heat to low. Simmer for 5 minutes, stirring occasionally. Spoon gravy over roast slices to serve.

Makes 8 to 12 servings.

Creamy Horseradish Sauce

A delicious addition to any roast beef dinner is this creamy horseradish sauce.

1 container (8 oz./250 g) sour cream
⅓ cup (75 mL) prepared white horseradish, drained (extra hot is best)
¼ cup (50 mL) mayonnaise
½ tsp. (2 mL) coarsely ground black pepper
1 tbsp. (15 mL) Dijon mustard

In a medium bowl, stir together all ingredients; cover and refrigerate until ready to serve.

For my friend Lily James, no roast beef could be served without Yorkshire puddings. Perhaps because she came from England, her popovers (as our American friends like to call them) are simply the best. Although Lily passed away many years ago now, I think of her each time I eat these "melt in your mouth" puddings.

Yorkshire Pudding

2 eggs
1 cup (250 mL) milk
1 cup (250 mL) sifted flour
½ tsp. (2 mL) salt
2 tbsp. (30 mL) water
vegetable oil

1. Beat eggs until frothy. Add milk and, with an electric mixer, beat in flour, salt and water. The batter should be slightly runny. Refrigerate and chill thoroughly.
2. Place about 1 tbsp. (15 mL) of oil in each cup of a large-size 12-cup muffin pan. Heat in a 425°F

(220°C) oven. Lily told me that the secret to the best Yorkshire pudding is to use very hot oil. Remove pan and half-fill the muffin cups with batter. (If the batter seems a bit too thick, add a little cold water to thin it.)

3. Place muffin pan on the centre rack in the oven and bake until puddings are puffed and golden brown (about 20 minutes).
4. Serve with a spoonful of hot gravy over each and listen to everyone rave about them!

Although I could make my Christmas meal with just turkey and stuffing, the rest of the family insists that we serve other dishes. Potatoes are well-loved in our family and I offer several recipes for your enjoyment.

Mashed Potato and Chive Casserole

12 to 14 medium potatoes
½ cup (125 mL) milk
¼ cup (50 mL) butter
8 oz. (250 g) cream cheese, softened
16 oz. (500 g) sour cream
¼ cup (50 mL) chopped chives
salt and pepper
whole chives for garnish

1. Peel potatoes and cook in boiling water until tender. Remove from heat and drain.
2. Add milk and butter and mash until potatoes are lump-free. Using an electric mixer, blend in cream cheese, sour cream and chives. Add salt and pepper to taste.
3. Transfer potato mixture to a serving dish. Garnish it with whole chives and serve immediately. If desired, potato mixture can be transferred to a glass casserole and refrigerated until needed. To serve, heat in microwave and garnish with whole chives.

Makes 8 to 10 servings.

Sweet Potato Casserole

We make such a large quantity because it is every bit as good as a leftover the next day.

6 or 7 large sweet potatoes (about 4½ lb. / 2 kg)
2 large eggs, lightly beaten
⅔ cup (150 mL) firmly packed brown sugar
½ tsp. (2 mL) ground nutmeg
⅔ cup (150 mL) milk
4 tbsp. (60 mL) butter or margarine, melted

2 tsp. (10 mL) vanilla extract
½ tsp. (2 mL) salt

TOPPING
1 cup (250 mL) firmly packed brown sugar
½ cup (125 mL) all purpose flour
4 tsp. (20 mL) butter or margarine, cut up
⅔ cup (150 mL) chopped pecans

1. Preheat oven to 250°F (180°C). Peel the sweet potatoes, cut them in small pieces, and put them in a pot containing enough water to cover them. Boil until potatoes are soft. Drain and mash.
2. In a large bowl, stir together the mashed potatoes, beaten eggs, brown sugar, nutmeg, milk, melted butter or margarine, vanilla and salt.
3. Spoon mixture into a lightly greased 9" × 13" (22 × 23 cm) baking dish.
4. To make the topping, combine brown sugar and flour, then cut in butter with a pastry blender until the mixture is crumbly. Stir in pecans and sprinkle mixture over the sweet potato mixture. Bake for 30 minutes.

Makes 14 to 16 servings.

Green Beans with Bacon and Almonds

Although most of the children would prefer to skip the vegetables, nearly all of them will eat this green bean dish.

4 slices bacon
⅓ cup (75 mL) sliced almonds
2 lbs. (1 kg) fresh or frozen green beans
2 tbsp. (30 mL) butter
¼ tsp. (1 mL) garlic powder
½ tsp. (3 mL) lemon pepper

1. Cook bacon in a skillet or microwave until crispy. Place on paper towel to drain, then crumble the pieces. Set aside.
2. Place sliced almonds on a cookie sheet and toast in a 325°F (160°C) oven for about 2 minutes or until crispy. Remove from oven and set aside.
3. Cook green beans in boiling water until just tender. Drain. Melt butter over the beans. Add garlic powder, lemon pepper, almonds and bacon and toss together. Serve immediately.

Makes 8 servings.

Snow Peas with Water Chestnuts

This unusual but very tasty dish is a light addition to a large meal.

½ lb. (250 g) fresh or 2 pkgs. (6 oz./145 g each) frozen snow peas
1 tbsp. (15 mL) butter or margarine
½ can (4 oz./125 g) sliced water chestnuts, drained
1 clove garlic, finely minced
½ tsp. (2 mL) salt
½ tsp. (2 mL) pepper
½ tsp. (2 mL) lemon juice

1. If using fresh snow peas, wash them thoroughly and trim the ends. If using frozen peas, defrost and drain on paper towels.
2. Melt butter in a large skillet. Add the snow peas, water chestnuts, garlic, salt, pepper and lemon juice. Cook over medium high heat, stirring continuously until vegetables are tender but still crunchy. Serve immediately.

Makes 4 servings.

With all of the rich food that is served with the Christmas dinner, it's nice to have a light salad that young and old enjoy. The following recipes are just right.

Jell-O Mould

1 pkg. orange Jell-O
1 container (8 oz./250 g) of small-curd cottage cheese
1 container (8 oz./250 g) of Cool Whip
1 can (15 oz./420 g) crushed pineapples, drained
1 can Mandarin orange sections, drained

1. Mix dry Jell-O powder with the cottage cheese and Cool Whip.
2. Add the pineapple and oranges, stirring gently to mix. Pour into a decorative mould and refrigerate until ready to serve.

Makes 8 to 10 servings.

Cranberry-Apple Salad

1 medium thin-skinned orange, cut into 8 sections (seeds removed)
1 medium apple, cored, peeled and cut into 8 sections
2 cups (500 mL) fresh or frozen cranberries
1¼ cup (300 mL) sugar
1 small package orange or lemon Jell-O
1 envelope unflavoured gelatin
1 cup (250 mL) cold water
grated peel and juice from 1 lemon

1. Using a food chopper or a blender, finely chop orange, apple and cranberries. Add sugar and mix well. Refrigerate, stirring occasionally, to dissolve the sugar, for 2 hours or overnight.
2. Prepare the Jell-O according to the package directions.
3. In a small saucepan, soften the unflavoured gelatin in the cold water. Cook over low heat, stirring until dissolved. Add to Jell-O along with lemon peel and juice. Chill until it is the consistency of unbeaten egg whites.
4. Fold in the fruit mixture until thoroughly blended. Pour into a 6-cup (1.5 L) ring mould. Chill until

firm. When ready to serve, unmould onto a serving plate and garnish with Frosted Cranberries.

FROSTED CRANBERRIES

In a small bowl, lightly beat 1 egg white. Dip 1 cup (250 mL) of cranberries in egg white, then roll each cranberry in granulated sugar to coat. Let dry at least 30 minutes before using.

Makes 8 to 10 servings.

As our family sits around the Christmas dinner table, our conversation invariably turns to memories of Christmases past. My great-grandchildren enjoy hearing me tell of riding in horse-drawn sleighs or of going carolling from house to house. We all have interesting or humorous events that spring to mind but my grandson Fred and his wife, June, never fail to send us all into gales of laughter with this next story.

A Doggone Mess

Fred and June live with their two sons, Mickey and Geoffrey, in a rural area in Southern Ontario. Because they have a large property, their pet population has always been sizable. Cats, dogs, rabbits and even a horse have enjoyed a very comfortable home with much love from the family. One year, when the boys were still quite young, one of their dogs, a yellow Lab, had puppies. Eight adorable puppies were born in mid-September and, June reasoned, they would be ready to go to loving homes right around Christmastime. Was there ever a better present for someone than a wonderful, fun-loving puppy?

The puppies were all healthy and growing at a rapid rate. At first the young animals stayed in the barn, but as the weather grew colder, the barn (which was unheated) was no longer the best place to keep them. To the boys' delight, Fred and June made a bed for them in the basement of their home. The basement was unfinished and the dogs had the run of the entire area.

As it came closer to Christmas, all of the eight puppies had been sold; however, since six of the pups were being delivered by Santa, Fred and June agreed to keep the young animals until Christmas Eve.

Fred and June were having the whole family for Christmas dinner and June had done a masterful job of decorating. Never had a tree looked so beautiful! The gifts were exquisite and the house was spotlessly clean and ready to entertain our large family group.

Early on the morning of Christmas Eve, June remembered that she needed more milk. Fred was at work, so June and the boys jumped into the car and headed into town.

What happened next is not entirely clear. Perhaps the door to the basement was left open . . . or maybe one of the pups simply pushed his little nose up against the door hard enough that it opened. However it happened, all six puppies escaped the confines of the cellar and spent the next two hours romping through the entire house.

When June and the boys arrived home, the scene was nearly unbelievable.

"At first," said June, "I was ready to call the police. I assumed that we had had a break-in and the house had been ransacked. Just then, one of the puppies who had heard our arrival came racing across the kitchen floor . . . a ribbon dangling from her mouth and bits of wrapping paper stuck to her tiny claws. The rest of the pups, equally excited to know that we were home, came rushing to the kitchen to greet us. One of the little ones looked especially festive as silver tinsel dangled from her ears and tail. I didn't know whether to laugh or cry but when the two boys started laughing, I did too. What a mess! It took us all day to clean up what the dogs had done but every time I'd begin to get angry, I pictured the little tinsel-decorated animal and I would laugh myself silly. Fortunately, I had film in my camera and we were able to record the event for posterity. The boys and I still get a kick out of looking at that scrapbook."

And we still love to hear that story!

I don't know about your family but for us, dessert holds a very special place in our hearts. In particular, any dessert that contains chocolate is very near and dear. This next recipe is definitely one to cherish if you are a chocolate lover.

Chocolate Lover's Cake

5 oz. (140 g) unsweetened chocolate
⅔ cup (150 mL) butter or margarine
1⅔ cup (400 mL) all-purpose flour
½ cup (125 mL) unsweetened cocoa powder
1½ tsp. (7 mL) baking soda
½ tsp. (2 mL) salt

3 eggs
1¾ cups (425 mL) sugar
2 tsp. (10 mL) vanilla extract
1⅔ cups (400 mL) buttermilk

1. Preheat the oven to 350°F (180°C). Coat two 9" (22.5 cm) cake pans with cooking spray. In a pot on low heat, melt the chocolate with the butter. Remove from heat and set aside.
2. In a bowl, combine flour, cocoa, baking soda and salt. Set aside.
3. In a bowl, beat the eggs with an electric mixer on high speed until eggs are pale and thick (3 to 4 minutes). Reduce speed to low and gradually beat in sugar and vanilla. Beat in the flour mixture and buttermilk alternately until mixture is well combined.
4. Add chocolate mixture and combine well. Increase speed to medium and beat for 1 minute.
5. Divide the batter into the two pans. Bake for 25 to 30 minutes or until a knife comes out clean. Cool on racks for 15 minutes before removing from pans. Cool cake completely before frosting.

FILLING AND FROSTING
1½ pkgs. (18 oz./500 g) semi-sweet chocolate pieces
¾ cup (175 mL) half and half cream

1½ cups (375 mL) butter
1½ lb. (680 g) confectioner's sugar
extra chocolate for decorative curls

1. In a medium saucepan, over medium heat, combine chocolate pieces, cream and butter. Cook, stirring until mixture is smooth.
2. Transfer mixture to a large mixing bowl; with electric mixer on high speed, beat in confectioner's sugar.
3. Place bowl in a larger bowl of ice and water and beat frosting at high speed until frosting is firm enough to spread. With a metal spatula, cover the top of first layer of cake. Place second layer on top and cover top and sides of the whole cake.

   Decorate the top of the cake with chocolate curls if you like.

Charlotte Russe

A wonderful Christmas dessert, Charlotte Russe looks beautiful and tastes just as good as it looks.

2 envelopes unflavoured gelatin
½ cup (125 mL) cold water

7 egg yolks
1 cup (250 mL) sugar
2 cups (500 mL) milk
½ tsp. (2 mL) almond extract
2 tsp. (10 mL) vanilla extract
4 cups (1 L) frozen whipped topping, thawed
2 pkgs. (6 oz. / 170 g) ladyfingers
2 pints (500 mL) fresh raspberries
¼ cup (50 mL) sifted powdered sugar

1. Sprinkle gelatin over the cold water. Let stand for 1 minute.
2. In a heavy saucepan, beat egg yolks and sugar with an electric mixer on medium speed until the mixture is thick and pale (3 to 4 minutes).
3. Heat milk over low heat until just warm and add to the egg mixture in a slow, steady stream, whisking constantly. Cook mixture over low heat, whisking constantly, for 5 to 7 minutes or until the mixture coats the spoon. Remove from heat. Add gelatin to the mixture, stirring until the gelatin dissolves.
4. Stir in almond and vanilla extracts and then pour the custard mixture into a metal mixing bowl. Place the bowl in a larger bowl of water and ice and let the mixture stand for 8 to 10 minutes (stirring often) or until the custard is slightly thickened.

5. Fold the whipped topping gently into the custard.
6. Line the side of a bowl—ideally a glass bowl with a flat bottom—with ladyfingers and pour in the custard mixture. Refrigerate for about 8 hours (or overnight). Cover the top of the custard with fresh raspberries and sprinkle with the sifted powdered sugar.

Makes 12 servings.

GLORIA IN EXCELSIS DEO
Carole Black

A Christmas Farewell

Christmas is such a wonderful time of year. It's a time of hope, of joy and a time when wishes come true. With that in mind, I have special wishes for you all.

May you have:
Enough happiness to keep you sweet,
Enough trials to keep you strong,
Enough sorrow to keep you human,
Enough hope to keep you happy,
Enough failure to keep you humble,
Enough success to keep you eager,
Enough friends to give you comfort,
Enough wealth to meet your needs,
Enough enthusiasm to look forward,
Enough faith to banish depression,
And enough determination to make each day better than yesterday.

Merry Christmas to you all!
Edna McCann

List of Christmas Carols and Decorations

CHRISTMAS CAROLS

CHRISTMAS DECORATIONS

Index